A PARE
GUIDE
PRIMARY
SCHOOL

Elizabeth Grahamslaw

To my children, Benjamin and Hannah, who taught me all I know.

This edition published in Great Britain in 2006 by
Virgin Books Ltd
Thames Wharf Studios
Rainville Road
London
W6 9HA

First published in Great Britain in 2004 by Virgin Books Ltd

A catalogue record for this book is available from the British Library.

ISBN 0 7535 1107 X
ISBN 9 780753 511077

The paper used in this book is a natural, recyclable product made from wood grown in
sustainable forests. The manufacturing process conforms to the regulations of the country
of origin.

Typeset by Phoenix Photosetting, Chatham, Kent
Printed and bound in Great Britain by Clays Ltd, Bungay, Suffolk

CONTENTS

ACKNOWLEDGEMENTS

I would like to thank the following for their help with researching this book: Wheatcroft Community Primary School, St Martin's Church of England Primary School, Braeburn Infant and Nursery School, Raincliffe School, all Scarborough; Dr Sandy Seton-Browne, consultant child and adolescent psychiatrist; Diane Quinney of the Workers' Educational Association; North Yorkshire School Library Service; and the Department for Education and Skills.

INTRODUCTION

There's nothing quite like your child's first day at school, that gut-twisting feeling when your four-year-old waves you goodbye and sets off alone on the road to independence.

For them and for you it's an enormous step, a leap, like it or not, into the relentless whirlpool of modern education. Daunting, certainly, but for the clued-up parent, an opportunity no previous generation has ever had.

Gone forever are the bad old days when parents felt as welcome in the classroom as an outbreak of chickenpox. Now the enormous contribution parents make to their children's education has finally been recognised.

Schools are crying out for parents to become more involved and the mysteries of education are mysteries no more. Show an atom of interest and teachers will welcome you with open arms. They'll show you how to teach your child to read, how to write and, surely the greatest mystery of all time, how to link the words 'maths' and 'fun'.

The more you know about how schools work, the more you and your child can enjoy those crucial early years.

This comprehensive guide to state education will tell you all you need to know, from the sticking and gluing extravaganza of the pre-school days to the nerve-jangling finale of those dreaded national tests. It also takes a separate look at the main differences between the education systems in England, Scotland, Wales and Northern Ireland. While the advice and information in this guide will help parents everywhere, all schools and the education authorities that run them have their differences. For more information on regional variations, see Chapter 22.

While this book will have particular appeal to mothers, I hope it will also be read by the growing number of fathers who play a huge part in the upbringing and education of their children. Also, please note that though I mainly refer to the individual child as 'he' and to teachers often as 'she', this is purely for consistency.

A Parents' Guide to Primary School will help you keep the whole scary business of education in perspective. This is a feet-on-the-ground guide for parents who believe that children are not just learning machines and that they should actually be allowed some fun.

So, be daunted no more. Welcome to the world of education.

1 PRE-SCHOOL

A successful first step on the learning ladder starts long before your child ever goes to school.

For the first two years of his life, you are his main teacher. The more you talk to your child, play with him and involve him in your world, the more he'll learn. And if that sounds obvious, then count your family among the lucky ones. You'd be amazed how many children start school unable to hold a conversation because they're not used to being spoken to at home. Sadder still, perhaps, is the number of children who have to be taught how to build a Duplo tower because they've never learned to play.

But, however conscientious you are with the home-made play dough and Kipper's invaluable A–Z, the time will come when the most important lesson your child has to learn can only be learned without you. Pre-school education will teach your child many things, but none more important than how to get by without mum or dad.

The moment you slip out of that nursery door, whether with a tear in your eye or a whoop of celebration, your child has to start thinking for himself in a way he never would with you around. He has to decide what to play with, who to play with, and whether to raise the roof when some child he has never met before snatches all the carriages off his Brio train.

So, yes, your child will learn about shapes and colours and make weird and wonderful models from an old box of chocolates and a yogurt pot. But never underestimate the most valuable lesson of all. A pre-school that turns your self-centred, can't share, won't share, three-year-old into a child who can listen to a story, stand up in front of his peers to be the fourth currant bun in a baker's shop, go two hours without you and still come home in the same pants, *and* resist the temptation to thump the great Brio train robber has served your child well.

A big thumbs up then for pre-schools, but which one do you pick? It may seem confusing, but choosing is probably a lot simpler than you might think. Remember that in these days when rules and regulations verge on the obsessive, most pre-schools are regulated by Ofsted (the schools inspectors) and are aiming to teach your child pretty much the same as each other.

Where they differ is in approach. Some are unnervingly like school – desks, uniforms, the lot – while others appear at first glance a free-for-all largely involving glue, paint, water and a vaguely greyish pastry. So, will your child be happiest at a desk or up to his elbows in sand and clay? You decide.

THE MAIN OPTIONS

State-run nurseries: Most of these are attached to primary schools, while others mop up children from various catchment areas without designated nurseries of their own. Starting age tends to be around three or four.

Pros: The big bonus of a nursery attached to a school is that your child will mix largely with children he'll be with right through primary school. He'll have a whole circle of friends before school even starts. The transition to school proper should be a breeze.

Cons: Lack of flexibility. State nursery schools tend to be a five half-days a week commitment, tying you to a rigid and, for some young-sters, exhausting timetable when your child may be barely three. Some would say there's more to life for a three-year-old.

Pre-schools/playgroups: Tend to be run by volunteer committees that employ the staff, though some are businesses run for profit. Many are based in church halls and community centres and are committed to the idea of learning through play. Children, often accepted from the age of two-and-a-half, are generally encouraged to take part in activities rather than coerced. Parents can usually book as many or as few half-day sessions as they choose. Not all are open all day or all week, but some provide longer hours for parents who want them.

Pros: Most feel part of their community and welcome parental involve-ment. Rotas for parent helpers are common. You have been warned.

Cons: Some are restricted by their premises. It can be tricky to set up and store equipment like computers when you have to be out by noon so the Townswomen's Guild can come in at 2 p.m.

Day nurseries: Often run privately as businesses, sometimes set up by employers to benefit their staff, but can be run by a variety of agencies.

They appeal particularly to working parents. Most accept children from babies upwards and offer the option of long hours.

Pros: Where profits depend on impressing parents, expect plenty of facilities and lots of gloss. A godsend for many working parents.

Cons: Not everyone's idea of an ideal childhood for children who are there all day, every day. Can be expensive.

Private nursery schools: Often the top end of the market. Some are independent businesses, some are attached to public schools.

Pros: Good facilities, qualified teachers, often good wrap-around care which might, for instance, involve a child staying for lunch.

Cons: Can be formal, which won't suit every boisterous three-year-old. Fees can be high.

Registered childminders: Some specially accredited childminders provide pre-school education for the children in their care. Accredited childminders, who are always part of a childminding network, can claim the government grants available for pre-school education, but are subject to Ofsted inspections and have to provide a standard of education children would otherwise get at nursery.

Pros: Children are taught in very small groups. Can appeal to parents who want continuity of care rather than have their child get used to both nursery and childminder.

Cons: There are still relatively few accredited childminders and they may be particularly hard to find in some areas. Won't in itself get children used to mixing in bigger groups – though other activities organised by the childminder may.

MAKING YOUR CHOICE

Make appointments to visit all the pre-school providers you are considering. Ideally, go without your child so that you can concentrate on what the nursery has to offer.

Points to consider:

1. The practicalities. Will this work around your other commitments? Is there any wrap-around care to fit in with your working hours?
2. The location. Even the best playgroup in town has disadvantages if it's so far from where you live that your child will still go to one school while all his new friends go to another.
3. The atmosphere. Does it look like school before school even starts? Does it look chaotic? Is there enough for children to do? Are the

quiet ones drawn in? Do the children look happy? Do the children look bored?

4. The staff. Do they have a good rapport with the children? Do they have fun with them? How do they deal with children who are not behaving well?

5. The surroundings. Pre-schools should look bright and breezy, colourful and enticing. There should be artwork on the walls and intriguing toys to play with. But as for the rest, don't set too much store by it looking like something from Ikea. If there's sand on the floor and chips in the paintwork it's probably a sign that the children are actually allowed some fun.

6. The cost. If your child is three or older, current funding arrangements in England mean that you will get some, if not all, of your child's pre-school education for free. You can claim for up to five half-day sessions. Expect to pay for wrap-around care and pre-school education for younger children.

7. The timetable. Don't be steamrollered into five sessions a week unless that suits your child and your family. Some children can't get enough of nursery, but not all. Rest assured, he won't fail his GCSEs just because you booked three mornings instead.

Finally, remember that pre-school childcare in its many guises is hyper-competitive. Lots of different businesses and organisations want your child and the education authority grants that come with him. So dismiss the sales patter and think about your own child. Ask yourself, could he be happy here? If the answer is yes, book a trial morning. Try to stand back and see how he gets on.

Don't be surprised if there are a few tears at the start, but if after a fortnight he's going in happy and coming out happy – if a tad gluey – you've probably cracked it.

A teacher once said to me that you could spot a mile off the children who had been to playgroup. It's the way they cope with sharing, sitting quietly on the mat for a story, how they do the tasks they're given, all that carries through to school. They arrive receptive to learning.

The mother of a six-year-old boy

The friendships that form at playgroup can last throughout their time at primary school. My nine-year-old is still in the same group of friends he made at playgroup when he was three.

A mum of three

---

2 WHAT YOUR CHILD SHOULD LEARN *BEFORE* STARTING SCHOOL

The closer school looms, the greater the sense of parental paranoia.

It would take a parent with nerves of steel not to feel a tinge of panic that theirs will be the only child in reception who can't recognise every letter of the alphabet and still thinks the number that looks like a little duck is four.

There's that sinking, churning, not-done-your-homework feeling for mums and dads about the whole scary business of going back to school. It's often at this stage that even the most laid-back of parents can't resist putting a toe into the hothouse in a bid to ensure that their child gets off to a flier.

Suddenly, the word 'educational' stamped on anything draws them like a vortex. They buy educational children's magazines, play educational games, do educational jigsaws and take up residence at the oh-so-educational children's library. And all this so that, on day one, their conscience will be clear as they enter the dreaded classroom with a child who has finally grasped the link between 'a' and 'ant'.

For some, there's more than an element of showing off as they introduce their child to his school.

'He knows all his times tables up to four,' one mother boasted to the reception teacher on her son's first day. And, indeed, he did, could recite the lot without hesitation. The only problem was, he had not the remotest idea what any of it meant.

Yet if you ask what is a realistic level for your child to aim for by the time he starts school, you'll like as not get a wishy-washy reply. And the reason? Confusingly enough, children start school in a no-man's land, halfway up the bottom rung on the learning ladder.

The foundation stage comes before the first key stage of the national curriculum proper gets under way. Three- to five-year-olds work their way through various learning goals in their pre-school or nursery and continue that same learning programme in the reception class at primary school. The aim is that by the time they join Year 1, children should have the basic skills they need to tackle the first key stage of the national curriculum.

This is all very well, but not terribly helpful to you as a parent trying to grasp what your child should ideally know *before* he goes to school.

So just what would make a reception teacher's day? Opinions vary, but be assured that you're on the right track if your child:

- Can recognise numbers up to five
- Knows the main colours
- Can write his own first name
- Recognises *some* letters
- Holds a pencil properly
- Can dress himself
- Is able to count a set of objects

And if he can't? Don't worry. All children are individuals and they all develop at different rates. Just as some children walk before others, so some children are ready to learn long before their peers and some take that bit longer. You are about to hand your child over to the experts. They know every trick in the book to help guide both you and him through the early days of learning.

Worry, by all means, if thirteen years from now you can't get him to swot for his A levels. But he hasn't even got to school yet. Now, trust us, is not the time to worry.

TIPS FOR GETTING YOUR CHILD READY TO LEARN

The dream pupil for a reception teacher isn't necessarily the child who arrives knowing the most, it's the child who's fired up on the starting blocks, equipped with all the skills he'll need to learn.

A child who has had one-to-one intensive tuition from a particularly eager mum may flounder at school if he hasn't learned the basics he'll need to survive in a busy classroom.

Social skills are vital. Unless children know how to co-operate with their classmates, unless they've been taught to share and have some basic good manners, their first year at school is going to be a very steep learning curve indeed.

But the absolute secret to learning is listening, and that's another tough lesson for any four-year-old who, as they all do, comes pre-programmed to talk at volume nine. Getting your child to stop talking, listen, concentrate, understand, remember and act on instructions is a vital part of learning.

Ask him to practise talking in a 'little voice'. Challenge him to talk to you in a grown-up, sensible voice that isn't yelled from one end of the house to the other. Reciprocate by doing the same yourself, even if that means a blanket ban on shouting, 'Come on! Breakfast's on the table!' in a voice that rattles the china in the semi next door.

Get him into the habit of taking information on board and carrying it through. Stop what you're both doing, explain clearly and with lots of eye contact that you want him to go upstairs now, go into the top drawer in his bedroom, choose a pair of blue socks, and put them on.

If he manages all that without veering off to play with Action Man or choosing the Bart Simpson pair, not only will you have started to prepare him for that multitude of complex instructions he'll face from his teacher, you'll also have the satisfaction of knowing that you've just achieved a minor miracle.

HELPING YOUR CHILD AT HOME

There are lots of activities you can do at home to support the good work being done in nursery and reception classes.

READING

There's something very special about reading to a small child. Whether you're cuddling on the settee or snuggled up in bed, sharing a book with a child is one of the great pleasures of parenthood.

It is also one of the key ways you can prepare your child for the challenges of learning to read that lie ahead.

All the time you're reading, your child is learning about how to turn pages, how print reads from left to right and from top to bottom. He's expanding his vocabulary as you talk about what's happening in the pictures. He's using his imagination by guessing what might happen next. He's learning about rhyming words, stretching his memory, recognising letters.

And, oh, joy unbounded, he also gets to laugh raucously at your downfall if you slip the odd mistake into his favourite story.

The time you spend reading to your child is one of the biggest investments you can make in his development. It's impossible to overplay its value.

So, don't rush it. Far better to take your time reading one story, talking about the pictures and doing the funny voices, than to read six stories at a lick.

It's a lovely way to take a break in a busy day. Books are too precious to save only for bedtime.

WRITING

Encourage your child to be aware of what writing is and what it's used for. The more he sees you writing notes, lists and letters, the more he will see the value and use of writing. And if you can get him writing, too, so much the better.

Ask for his help in writing, for instance, a shopping list. Can he draw some of the items you might need? Can he copy a 'c'? Can he hear the 'c' sound that starts 'cake'? Remember, what you need him to learn is letter *sounds*; letter names won't help a child to learn to read.

Encourage him to write, even if his scribbles on a page are play-writing. Ask him to tell you what his writing says. Odds on, he'll have a go at telling you – and so start to realise that writing carries a message.

Once he is holding a pencil properly and his 'writing' contains shapes you recognise, you can start to teach him how to write letters. Writing his own first name is a good place to start. He'll want a capital letter at the start, of course, but then teach him small letters. It's the small letters children learn first in the classroom.

MATHS

Working with numbers is going to be a big part of your child's school life right from the start. Even those of us who found maths a complete trial at school should really try to muster up some enthusiasm the second time around.

Counting songs are an easy way to set the ball rolling. Yes, one day you really will be pleased you put up with 'One, Two, Three, Four, Five ...' on that nerve-grating children's tape he always wants on in the car.

And the weekly trip to the supermarket is an excellent maths resource.

Get him to count five oranges into a bag then change your mind and ask for one more. How many are there now?

Let him choose a baking potato, then ask for a bigger one. Can he reach the onions behind the parsnips? Can he choose four carrots from the box in front of the cabbages?

All good practice for the basic language and basic skills he'll need in his early maths lessons. And while it'll probably take you twice as long to reach the checkout, look on the bright side. He'll be far too distracted to paddy when you pull a fast one and skirt past the chocolate aisle.

At home, give him practical tasks involving numbers. How many spoons will he need to put on the table if everyone in the family is having ice cream?

And any kind of sorting is a great way of getting ready for maths proper. Can he take a lead from Goldilocks and find a big bear, a middle-sized bear, and a baby bear among his toys? Can he sit them in size order? Can he make a tower with only green bricks? Can he finish your pattern if you create a toy traffic jam with alternating red and blue cars?

There you go, you see. You've forgotten you're doing maths already.

WHAT YOUR CHILD WILL LEARN

In pre-school and reception classes in England, staff will be focused on guiding your child through the Foundation Stage curriculum. It has six areas of learning, all judged equally important. Within them are a number of early learning goals, targets most children are expected to achieve by the end of their reception year in school.

The six learning areas are:

Personal, social and emotional development: Your child will be encouraged to grow in self-confidence, take an interest in things, know his own needs, understand the difference between right and wrong, and be able to dress and undress.

Communication, language and literacy: Your child will read and write some familiar words and learn to use a pencil. He should talk confidently and clearly, enjoy stories, songs and poems, hear and say sounds, and learn the link between sounds and the alphabet.

Mathematical development: Stories, songs, games and imaginative play will all boost your child's understanding of maths. He will feel at ease with numbers and ideas such as 'bigger' or 'heavier than', and will learn all about shapes and space.

Knowledge and understanding of the world: Your child will explore and ask questions to increase his understanding of the world around him. He will build with different materials, learn about everyday technology and discover what it's used for. He will be encouraged to find out about past events in his life and his family's lives. He will learn about different cultures and beliefs.

Physical development: The aim is to encourage your child to move confidently, controlling his body and handling equipment.

Creative development: A chance to explore colours and shapes, try out dance, make things, tell stories and make music.

Daunting? Well, for you, perhaps, but for the children, hardly. Most of the time, it'll just seem like playing.

So, relax. The pressure is off. These are the fun years. Let him enjoy them while he can.

3 CHOOSING A SCHOOL

Choosing your child's first school is a tough decision. For most families, this is our first experience of school as a parent, and the first decision we're asked to make is one of the hardest.

How do you go about choosing a school when it might be twenty years since you last stepped in one? How are you supposed to have a clue what you're looking for when education has undergone a sea change since your own school days? And what difference will your decision make anyway if all children study from the national curriculum? Surely, they'll learn the same wherever they go.

Well, yes, but school is so much more than the literacy hour. School brings with it a whole new social circle for your child, it instils a set of values that will influence his outlook, and it has the power to implant in him a zest for learning – or turn him off education altogether.

The child you send in is probably the most important being in the universe to you. You need to find a school that will treat your child as an individual, somebody who matters, not just another source of income from the education authority and a potential high scorer in the national test results.

In theory, there should be lots of choice. In practice, for many of us there is less than we would want. If it were really so straightforward, we would doubtless all send our children to the nearest school with a glowing Ofsted report, league tables to die for, a flash IT suite, and children straight out of the pages of Enid Blyton.

But do your homework (sorry to mention the 'h' word so soon), plan your strategies, and you'll at least improve your chances of getting your child into a school you feel happy with. So, deep breath. Here's step one.

LOOKING AT THE OPTIONS

It's never too early to start considering your choices. At the risk of becoming obsessed, if you're moving into a new area or moving house it makes sense to suss out the local schools, even if your baby's first day at school is still four years away. Every parent will tell you how quickly those four years fly. And, while living in the catchment area won't necessarily guarantee you a school place, for many schools it'll almost certainly help.

It makes sense to start thinking about which school you might choose before you make a decision on pre-school. If the playgroup or nursery of your choice has strong links with your preferred school, it might help to secure you a school place as well as helping your child to form friendships that could carry over into his school days.

It's very important at this stage to put aside any preconceptions you may have. The school you swore you'd never send your child to might surprise you if you go to the bother of finding out what it's really like.

Don't be swayed by what parents tell you about a school their child doesn't attend. Opting for a school is a bit like choosing a football team. Once parents make their decision, they tend to become incredibly loyal to their choice. This isn't necessarily because they're always pleased with the school's performance, but because they want to believe they made the right decision and because they want to feel their child is part of a winning team.

It helps to confirm their conviction that they made the right choice if they hear bad things about other schools. Take rumours of bad behaviour or poor teaching with a pinch of salt unless you hear them from someone directly connected with the school.

Your best bet is to talk to parents whose children are already there. Are they happy? Are the children happy? What has pleasantly surprised them? But remember that they're likely to make it sound like classroom heaven unless you dig deeper. Always ask, what has disappointed them most? It might be an eye-opener.

ASK THE EXPERTS

For the conscientious parent, the truth is out there.

Whatever you think of Ofsted, the school inspectors (and it's probably best not to ask a teacher unless you've an hour or two to spare), the fact is that their reports are essential reading for parents.

Ofsted inspections of schools in England are extraordinarily thorough and often cuttingly honest. If they uncover problems, they don't mince their words in spelling them out. Similarly, if the school is performing well, an Ofsted report will single out its strengths.

The reports are readily available and relatively easy to understand. They're surprisingly jargon-free, littered with phrases such as 'good', 'commendable standards', 'particularly impressive', and 'unsatisfactory'. The full reports are huge, but the summaries will tell you all you need to know.

They'll give you a fair picture of how the school is managed, how pupils progress, what parents think of the school, how the children behave, and the standard of teaching. They'll also spell out whether this is a school on the up or whether standards have dropped since the last inspection.

You can look at copies of Ofsted reports via the internet at www.ofsted.gov.uk. Or ask the school for a copy. Get the school to send you a prospectus while they're at it. Look at what they have to offer and then look at how the information is presented. Does this look like a school that makes an effort to involve parents? Does it seem welcoming? Does it make you want to find out more?

Another good source of information is the controversial performance tables. Again, not a favourite among many teachers, but it would be interesting to know how many would look at the tables before choosing a school in a new area for their own child.

The table will show how children in the final year at primary school fared in their Key Stage 2 national curriculum tests, commonly known as SATs. You can access the information at www.dfes.gov.uk/performancetables/.

The biggest flaw in the system used to be that by looking at figures in isolation, you were not comparing like with like. A school coming midway down the table, for instance, might have done extraordinarily well by a class with more than its fair share of less-able children.

That flaw has now been addressed by giving schools a 'value added' measure. This basically calculates how much children have improved between their first SATs at seven years and their second at the age of eleven. And it gives proper credit for the first time to schools that are working miracles with a low-ability intake.

But no system is perfect. Schools with an intake of largely high-ability children could argue that it's difficult for them to gain a good 'value added' score. It's up to you as parents to look at the information and read between the lines.

FRIENDS AND FRIENDSHIPS

At the end of the day, it's unlikely to be statistics that sway your decision. A huge factor for most parents is the social side of school.

The fact is – and there's no easy way of saying this – that most of us are put off schools in run-down areas because we're worried about who our children will end up mixing with.

The school can be fantastic, it can have a value-added score that's off the scale, the teaching can be exemplary, the enthusiasm bouncing off the walls – but there's still playtime, and what happens then?

The great fear among parents is that the child they sent in, the cherub who thinks the four-letter 'f' word is 'fish', will emerge from school knowing a whole new colourful vocabulary which is more 'f' than phonics.

We look at our innocent child, whose only knowledge of aggression comes from *Thunderbirds*, and we imagine him caught up in a playground scuffle involving the local drug-dealer's lad and a five-year-old whose favourite film is *The Texas Chainsaw Massacre*.

One mother, faced with sending her child to a school in a notoriously run-down area, said she'd get him a place elsewhere or teach him at home.

'All right, so I'm being a snob,' she said. 'I know I am. But I'm not doing this for myself. I'm being a snob because that's in my child's best interests. And in my book that makes it OK.'

And this is what happens. Parents with the most committed ideals, those of us spared the trauma of the eleven-plus and the segregation of the secondary modern, tend to put our ideals aside when our own children come along.

You might be very principled. You might be prepared to put yourself in all kinds of situations because of your beliefs, but putting your own children into the firing line is something else. It sounds terribly sniffy, terribly middle class – 'We don't want our little Johnny mixing with the riffraff' – but how many parents find it easy to be holier-than-thou when it affects their own child?

You could, of course, send your child to a school with a poor reputation.

You could get on the governing body and work hard to make a difference, but little Johnny will probably be in employment before your efforts really pay off.

What happens in practice is that many parents don't stay within the system. Those who have a choice get their child into a different school. Some move house.

The schools that are popular and full generate money, which means they can continue to thrive. Those with a poor reputation lose pupils and the money that goes with them. In theory, this gives them the incentive to improve. All too often what really happens is that they're caught in a vicious downward spiral, while the affluent parents move on to invest their skills and enthusiasm in a school already awash with middle-class values. Ideal? Hardly.

YOUR CHILD, YOUR CHOICE

Of course, what no report or table can tell you is which school would best suit *your* child and *your* circumstances.

Much as we might admire your optimism, it's almost certainly no good setting your heart on a top state school thirty miles away that is already heavily oversubscribed and only takes children from its catchment area. You might as well wait for a win on the lottery and hope for a place at Eton.

Your shortlist should be small, practical and promising. There's no point in looking round a school that offers no realistic chance of a place.

Your obvious starting point is your local school. It's worth a tour, even if its reputation goes before it. Go along and judge for yourself.

Other options might be church schools, which put theology before geography (in their selection criteria if not on the curriculum). Or you might explore the possibility of village schools. Some, with places to spare, will take children from a wider area, but remember that for you this is a massive commitment. Not only might you have to drive a relatively long journey twice a day for years to come, with all that might mean for your employment prospects, but all your child's school friends will also live miles away. You'll be backwards and forwards for football practice, play rehearsals, tea with friends. Unless you always harboured ambitions to drive a taxi, this might not be the option for you.

Once you've got your shortlist, ring and ask to visit the school. If the head offers you an appointment, you're on your way. If he or she doesn't, you might want to consider making your shortlist one school shorter.

THE VISIT

Go prepared. Draw up a crib sheet of questions you'll want to ask. Areas you might want to cover include:

- **The induction process:** How will your child get to know his new school? Will his teacher visit his playgroup? Will he get a chance to visit the school? When will he start? Is there any flexibility over a start date for younger children who might, for instance, want to postpone starting school until after Christmas? Will all children do full days from the off or will the younger ones go for half-days?
- **Discipline:** How does the school deal with poor behaviour? How will it ensure your child is safe? What happens at lunchtimes?
- **SATs:** Ask about results by all means, but delve into how children, particularly the younger ones, are prepared for the big tests. Are the children set extra homework? Is there out-of-hours tuition? Or is this a school that believes in taking the pressure off seven-year-olds? Either way, the answers will speak volumes.
- **Class sizes:** Ask not only about the infant classes, but what happens in the juniors when class sizes often rise.
- **Staffing levels:** How many support staff are there? Classroom assistants are becoming an increasingly important part of school life. Their role is vital in giving teachers a chance to give intensive teaching time to different groups in the class while an assistant helps to keep the rest of the children on track with their own studies. Ask, too, about extra teaching staff. The more additional teachers the school employs over and above the number it needs per class, the more scope there is for giving extra help to children who need it.
- **Facilities:** What facilities does the school possess? Is there a computer suite, for instance, or a sports field? Is this school equipped with the kind of facilities you can envisage one day mattering to your child?
- **Communication:** How are parents involved in what happens at school?

THE TOUR

The most revealing part of your visit to a school should be the tour. Ask the head if they'll show you around. Remember that it's not the flash new toilet block you want to see, it's the classrooms – and not just the reception classroom either. Your four-year-old will be a junior before you know it. It would be a poor teacher who couldn't make a reception class look inviting, but it's just as important that you see what the classrooms are like for the nine-year-olds.

Remember, what you're trying to get is the feel of the place. Modern classrooms are not silent shrines to learning. There should be a busy noise, a bustle of children about their work.

What are the classroom displays like? Does the work displayed cover a range of abilities? Do you get the impression that all the children are valued, not just the ones who can do nice, joined-up writing and a recognisable picture?

Are the cloakrooms tidy? Is there litter in the playground? Does the place look cared for?

What about the head? What kind of rapport does he have with the children? Expect him to know their names – after all, he should do – but does he seem to know the children behind them?

Do any of the children offer help by, for instance, opening a door for you and stopping to let you pass? Is this a school that values good manners?

Don't be put off by:

- Groups of children working in corridors. Some of the best schools spend their money on extra teachers, not extra classrooms.
- Playtime. If you have the misfortune to witness a playground at playtime, don't be put off by the apparent mayhem. Unless you see somebody actually pinned up against a wall, rest assured that they all look pretty much like that.
- A glimpse of bad behaviour. When the head offers you a tour of his school, he has no control over what you might see. Children are children. Sometimes they misbehave. What should reassure you as a parent would be seeing bad behaviour dealt with quickly, firmly and fairly. Nothing makes children feel more secure.

> What would I look for if I was choosing a school for my child? That factor X, a feel for the place, that relationship between the children and the teachers, how people in the school speak to each other. Trust your own judgment, trust yourself.
>
> *A head teacher*

ADMISSIONS AND APPLICATIONS

It is essential that you are organised well in advance of your child's anticipated start date. You will normally need to apply for a primary school place long before your child's fifth birthday, because so many schools now admit four-year-olds.

The first step for schools in England is to find out who handles admissions – the local authority or the school itself. If the school you prefer deals with its own admissions, you may have to apply to the school direct. If the local education authority (LEA) is responsible, it's vital that you fill in an LEA admissions form stating your preference, even if this is for your second-choice school. If you don't, it's possible that your child will only be allocated a place once all those who did state a preference have been dealt with. By then, all the places at your local school could have been taken.

Some education authorities co-ordinate admissions for all the schools in their area, which makes things somewhat simpler. You only have to fill in one common application form, issued by the authority. The LEA will be able to tell you if a co-ordinated scheme operates in your area.

OH, FOR A PLACE IN THE RIGHT *SCHOOL* . . .

People will go to the most extraordinary lengths to ensure their child gets a place in what they perceive to be a good school.

One mother confessed that she refused to have unprotected sex with her husband until they had bought a house in a good catchment area. And every year countless families go to all the trouble of moving house solely in the hope of securing a coveted place in a popular school.

For some it's an elaborate and expensive charade. Many is the family who have uprooted, squeezed themselves – kids, cats, computers, the lot – into the only hopelessly cramped accommodation they could afford in a desirable catchment area, only to put up the 'for sale' sign and move back to somewhere cheaper and more spacious as soon as their child's name was indelibly on the right school register.

Unscrupulous, certainly, but for some a price worth paying. Living near to a school with a buoyant reputation has a big impact on property prices. Families clamour to live there, so the demand rises. That forces up house prices, brings more affluent families into the school and makes it more desirable still.

A recent report showed that some parents were paying nearly £50,000 extra to buy a home in the catchment area of a good school. There were even reported to be seven places in Britain where the difference between the price of a catchment area house and a typical house was 100% or more.

The hike is particularly noticeable where – as can happen – one side of a street falls into a different catchment area to the other. Families will pay thousands of pounds extra for an identical house to one opposite just because of the school.

And, if moving house sounds a little drastic, many parents are not averse to a little creative form-filling in the hopes of securing a place in a good school. Head teachers the country over will know of parents who used a grandparent's address as the child's supposed home, praying no one would notice until it was all too late.

Some go even further than that. A recent survey showed that nearly a third of head teachers at the country's leading state primary schools had been offered cash by parents for places. More than 30% of the 50 head teachers questioned reported being offered money or some other bribe in return for a place at their school.

One head teacher in London was said to have been offered £5,000 for a place, while others were offered slightly more subtle bribery in the form of offers of help. A parent might, for instance, offer the school free access to their information technology expertise – provided, of course, a place is found for their child.

Unfortunately, not all the requests are subtle. One head reported being threatened that there would be 'consequences' unless a place was found for a would-be pupil.

Some 70% of head teachers said they knew some parents lied in their applications, not least by supplying false addresses. One family gave an address that turned out to be an empty field. For schools, that means more work and more time wasted.

PLAYING BY THE RULES

The government's stance is that it wants as many parents as possible to obtain a place for their child at their preferred school. Most schools have enough places for each child who applies, but some are very popular and cannot possibly squeeze in all the children who want a place.

You can find out from the school whether it had more applications than places in the previous year. If it receives too many applications, the authority in charge of admissions will follow a set of rules to decide who will be offered a place.

The admission authority in England can be the local education authority or, in some cases (like some voluntary-aided schools such as church schools), the governing body.

Some commonly used rules for deciding who should be offered a place include whether or not:

- Your child has a brother or sister already at the school
- You live in the school catchment area
- There are particular social or medical reasons why your child should go to the school
- Your family go to church (in the case of voluntary-aided church schools)

To add to the complications, the rules differ from one admission authority to the next, but they are all compelled to state the order in which they will apply their rules and what they would use as a tie-breaker. So, for instance, if the first rule is catchment area, then children who live in the area served by the school should be given priority before anyone else is offered a place.

If your preferred school is particularly popular, it makes sense to look at these rules, which are readily available, and consider where they leave your child. Some admission authorities give priority to parents who make a school their first preference. If in doubt, ask. The school or education authority will be happy to help you through the maze.

Arrangements vary for when and how you should apply. Check with the school or local education authority.

If you are not offered a place at your preferred school or if you are unhappy with the place given to your child, you can appeal. Information on how to go about that should be given on the letter detailing the outcome of your application.

The result will depend on how strong a case you can muster, but more than an element of luck also creeps in.

An independent panel will hear your appeal, which generally goes through two stages:

1. The admission authority explains why it didn't offer you a place. It might, for instance, say that the classrooms are too small and increasing the number of pupils would be detrimental to all the children. The panel then rules whether there was a good reason for turning you down.

2. If the panel agrees that there was a good reason for refusing your application, it will then hear your side of the argument. This is your chance to list all the reasons why you think this school is the best for your child. You'll need to come up with special factors that justify your child getting in, something particular to you and your circumstances.

The panel then has to make a decision based on whether the benefits of your child going to the school you want, as opposed to the school you have been offered, outweigh the problems caused to the school by admitting another child. If the panel rules in your favour, the school has to offer you a place.

If you lose your appeal, you can ask the school to put your child on their waiting list, if it has one, and hope that a place will come free after the school year starts.

Be warned that the situation is even tougher if your admission is refused because an infant class has already reached its legal limit. The law limits the number of pupils in an infant class with one qualified teacher to a maximum of thirty. In this type of appeal, the panel can only look at two things.

1. Whether the admission authority stuck to its own rules. If it didn't, your appeal can succeed, but only if your child would have been accepted had the rules been properly applied.
2. Whether the admission authority acted unreasonably, which the courts have ruled means completely irrationally or not based on the facts of the case.

Now you know why parental choice isn't always all it's cracked up to be.

We did seriously think about sending our children to a private school, but I didn't want a school where it was all about achieve, achieve, achieve. I don't want that for my children. I want them to have a rounded social experience and a feel for what the real world is like. Yes, I want them to achieve academically, but I also want them to be happy.

Would I have felt the same if we lived in a less popular catchment area? No. It's not the school that would have bothered me, it would have been the peer group, that's where the children would have got most of their influences from.

The mother of a six- and a seven-year-old

CHURCH SCHOOLS

Church schools tend to be good schools. They often do well in league tables and have an excellent reputation.

For many years, long before education became as competitive as it is now, places in church schools have been highly prized. And parents have played – as some still do now – that silly game of enrolling their child into Sunday school, never to be seen in church again once the desired school place was secured.

There are almost as many myths and misunderstandings surrounding church schools as there are around the religions they stand for. If you plan to send your child to a church school, you should at least do them the courtesy of finding out exactly what they have to offer.

There are, of course, many different religions and different schools. But for many parents contemplating a church school, the main options they will consider are Anglican or Roman Catholic, and it's those two we'll concentrate on here.

First, the myths.

All children in church schools are from professional families: Not true. Most will perhaps have more than their fair share of doctors and lawyers in the audience for the annual school play, but they'll be rubbing shoulders with single parents and disadvantaged families just as they would anywhere else.

You have to be a religious zealot to get in: Not true. It might help to go to church, but for many schools it's not a prerequisite of entry.

All church schools are heavily oversubscribed: Not true. Doubtless some are, but don't be put off even trying just because rumour has it they're always full. You might be surprised. At a time when churchgoing is in decline, some can't fill the places they've got.

So, just what can you expect if you opt to send your child to a church school? Well, as in schools everywhere, it depends. It can depend on the head, the governors, the parents, local church leaders, even, to some extent, geography. A Church of England school out in the middle of nowhere, for instance, which is the only realistic option for local families, may be less overtly religious than a town school to which parents choose to send their children.

Whether you have a faith or whether you have none, you owe it to your child and to yourself to find out exactly what happens in the church school you're considering. Ask about:

- Acts of worship. How often are they held and what do they involve? It might be a daily act of worship and a Bible story. In Catholic schools, it may sometimes be mass with communion.
- Religious teaching. How big a part of school life is absorbed by religious teaching, and what does it involve?
- Links with local churches. Some have very strong links with their local churches and lots of contact with their local vicar or priest.
- Admissions policy. Each school has its own policy and some put more emphasis on existing church links than others.

Try to go into the whole thing with an open mind, whichever side of the fence you fall. As well as following the national curriculum, any church school is likely to place great emphasis on the ethos of caring for each other and being kind, open and loving. Most parents would welcome that. Many would be happy with a teacher who wrapped her arms around a distressed child and told her that her dead hamster had gone to heaven.

Not all would be comfortable with the head who asked two boys, caught fighting in the playground, how Jesus would have reacted in the same situation.

This is why you need to do your homework. Many church schools will accept families from other faiths, and some will accept families of no faith at all. Children will be taught about religion, but there's no compulsion to join the club.

The only thing they probably all have in common is that the families they don't want are those who chose their school purely for its standing in the league tables. Yes, church schools often do very well by their pupils, but most are honest enough to admit that they are blessed with a largely good intake.

It isn't that these are exclusively children from the solicitors and doctors brigade, it's that the families who choose their schools – whether wealthy or not – tend to be very supportive. Some go to considerable inconvenience to send their children on what can be relatively long journeys to school. They are prepared to put themselves out for their children and that may be one of the biggest factors in their school's and their children's success.

If you do opt for a church school, you owe it to your child and the school to do it for the right reasons. You may have no faith yourself, but if you're going to send your child to a church school, with all that that will involve, you should at least let them make up their own minds about the messages you chose for them to hear.

4 GETTING READY FOR SCHOOL

Before you send your child to school, try kicking off your loafers and putting yourself in his little size 10 shoes. Imagine you're him.

It's your first day of school, you're 3ft small, lost in a playground of a seeming zillion trillion children, all bigger, all bouncier, all playing games you've never heard of because your mum thinks twenty minutes a day with the *Tweenies* is quite enough television for any four-year-old.

Think about the sheer terror of THE TOILET. What on earth will happen when your legs are plaited and *still* nobody tells you to go? What if you can't find the toilet? What if there is no toilet? What if – oh, horrors too terrible to contemplate – you wet those nice new trousers with the impossible zip.

Then there's gym, when for some reason no one has explained you have to take off almost all your clothes in the middle of the day and run around in your pants despite the fact that such clearly rude behaviour has been expressly forbidden since you were two. More alarming yet, there are buttons on your school T-shirt and the sweatshirt has a neck hole which you are sure is smaller than your head, because however hot it gets you would rather explode than face the public trauma of taking it off.

And if that sounds bad, imagine lunchtime when you swap that quiet chat with mum at the kitchen table for the seething chaos of the school dinner hall. Breathe in the smell, that overpowering gravy-cum-custard smell that turns your stomach.

And there you are, at the back of the queue, trying to find somewhere to sit and someone to sit with, someone who looks kind enough not to pass comment on the embarrassing *Bob the Builder* lunchbox your granny got in a sale. Finally, you're guided to a table by one of an army of schizophrenic dinner ladies who are so, so nice it almost feels like home ... until one of them rounds on a bigger boy guilty of the heinous crime of leaving a dirty tray at the table – from then on you make a mental note never to ask *them* for help with opening your Quavers.

Finally, you get around to the serious business of eating. You open the devilishly stiff clip on your new lunchbox and what do you find? That your mother, in that eager-to-impress stage of school-lunch preparations, has filled your box with tempting but inaccessible treats. There's a slightly-too-ripe banana with an impenetrable skin, a packet of crisps your sweat-soaked hands can't open, breadsticks and some houmous too cringeworthy to lift out of the box, and a Penguin welded into its wrapper. And what will your mum say later? 'Oh, Sam, you hardly ate any of your lunch!' So you pretend you weren't hungry to hide the shame.

Just what you need at the end of a day that has seemed longer than any day ever. 'Will my mum be coming soon?' you ask anybody who'll listen. 'Yes, soon,' they say.

But 'soon' turns out to be *ages* because you paint a picture and still she doesn't come. And you endure the traumas of the playground for the third time and still she doesn't come. And you hear a long, long story about a very hungry caterpillar (he thinks *he's* hungry) and still she doesn't come. And by the time she finally deigns to join all the other mums at the school gate you're so cross with her for leaving you so long that you could cry. And then you do, and what does she say? 'Don't cry. You're a big schoolboy now.' And you wish to goodness you weren't.

MAKING LIFE EASIER FOR YOUR CHILD

Don't panic. We can make starting school much less traumatic for children if we look at it through their eyes. So obsessed are we that they should do well, that they know their letters and can tot up their numbers, that we lose sight of the fact that learning is the last thing on their minds.

No child has ever started school worried that he can't tell his b's from his d's. Why would he worry about lessons? He has absolutely no idea what a lesson is. It's the little things that worry him – the fear of getting lost, the playtimes, the lunchtimes – but more, far more than all of these put together, the toilets.

So how can you make life easier for him?

- Always talk up school. Be positive whenever it comes up in conversation, even if in your heart of hearts it still feels like you're sending him to boot camp. Don't do that: 'Oh, I'm going to miss you so much,' social blackmail thing. It might be good for your morale – it might even earn you a hug – but it's terrible for his.

- On the other hand, don't get him so hyped up about school that it's bound to come as a big letdown. If he's been to nursery, the chances are that school will seem similar but with fewer toys. This is hardly good news for a four-year-old. If he goes in expecting wild excitement, he's going to be bitterly disappointed.
- Encourage him to dress and undress himself during the summer holidays when the time pressure is off. Resist the urge to leap in and help, or chip in words of encouragement along the lines of: 'Come on, you won't get this long when you're at school!'
- Don't buy shoes with laces that he won't be able to tie with confidence this side of puberty. Choose shoes with Velcro fasteners. A godsend to reception teachers everywhere.
- Practise so that your child can cope with all aspects – savoury and unsavoury – of going to the toilet alone. Teachers have many responsibilities these days, but bottom wiping is not among them. And make sure boys have been to a proper gents before they start school. Infant schools are awash with stories of boys who, never having seen a urinal before, dropped their trousers and sat in one on the first day or, worse still, washed their hands in one before lunch.
- Get out of the habit of zipping your child into his coat. Coat zips are tricky and unless he's mastered the art for himself he's going to have some hypothermic playtimes.
- Keep the lunchbox simple. He doesn't need a whole buffet in there. A sandwich, a piece of fruit and a treat if you can't resist it will be quite enough for him to cope with at first. Make life easy on the nervous diner by, for instance, scoring the skin at the top of a banana for easy access, and sticking a clothes peg on a pack of opened crisps. As for school dinners, does he really need the trauma of knives, forks, tray balancing and unknown concoctions in his first week? We think not.
- Put name-tags on everything. But even after all that fiddly sewing, accept from the off that there is nothing schoolchildren are incapable of losing. The day will come, sooner rather than later, when the pristine child you sent in comes home in a grubby looking sweatshirt you wouldn't send to a jumble sale that is clearly not his. Yes, it will take you a week to track down the one you lost. Yes, it will come back looking like it's been through a hot wash with a pint of ketchup and a muddy sheep, but smile serenely, thank the mother, then go and buy another. Uniforms tend, thankfully, to be ludicrously hard-wearing and mercifully cheap. This might be the first lost item you have to replace, but it certainly won't be the last.

WHEN SHOULD A CHILD START SCHOOL?

This is a very good question. Some parents would gladly send their children to school the week after they're toilet trained. Others would happily wait forever.

WHEN MUST A CHILD START SCHOOL?

All children in England (except where parents choose to educate at home) must be admitted into full-time education by the beginning of the term following their fifth birthday. In reality, many children start school much earlier.

Those with the misfortune to be born in the summer months often start school when they may be barely four. A child born on the last day of August may well have to start school a whole year ahead of a child born 24 hours later. And a year at this stage in a child's development is a very long time indeed.

How schools help such young children to cope is for them to decide. Some adopt a sink-or-swim attitude and all children go full-time from day one. Elsewhere, they take the view that children who scraped into that school year by a hair's breadth can't possibly be anything short of a zombie if they stay every day until 3.15 p.m.

They adopt policies designed to ease very young children into school gradually. Younger children might only do half-days until Christmas. Some schools even give parents the option of starting their children later in the school year. But for those dreading sending their children at all, that only opens up a whole new catalogue of dilemmas.

HOW DO I KNOW IF MY CHILD IS READY?

Are you thinking of keeping your child back because they aren't ready for school? Or is it because you're not ready to give them up? Many parents have agonised for weeks before making the decision.

How can you tell if your child is ready for school? Here you are with someone who still can't be trusted to get his *Thomas the Tank Engine* underpants on the right way round and you're supposed to wave him off into full-time education with confidence that he'll survive.

A month ago he was blowing out the four candles on his birthday cake and now both you and he are supposed to be ready for a life-changing separation. Can it be right?

All your instincts might scream at you to keep your child at home, but society is screaming just the opposite.

The education message is rammed down our throats from the moment our babies take their first breath. Such is the pressure on parents to push their children ever onward, that they can't even buy their new baby a rattle without reading on the side of the box about what it will do for their development.

Before you know it, they're in nursery two mornings a week, then three, then five, and all the time nagging away in the back of your mind is the fear that, unless your child seizes these opportunities, he'll be left behind, trampled underfoot by a tide of more competitive, more achieving parents and their super-brained children.

It would be a brave parent indeed who chose to keep their child out of school beyond the date decreed on the official admissions letter.

How could you bring yourself to enjoy an afternoon at the cinema or a kick around in the park imagining that his contemporaries were breezing their way through the finer points of long division and getting all the best speaking parts in the nativity?

Will all the other children know their letters? Will they be romping their way through the reading scheme? Just how far behind will he be?

And what about the social side of school? How can a child who starts school after Christmas possibly begin to fit in with a classroom full of children who've been getting used to this schooling lark since September? Who will look out for this late starter at playtimes? Who will help him when he's lost? Who will want to be his friend?

Oh, the dilemma. So many of us have been there. So many of us weakened and gave in.

But we probably based our final decision on irrational fears. School isn't like it was when we were young. A vast number of children change school not once, but several times during their childhood as job opportunities take their parents around the country. And because swapping schools isn't such an issue any more, it's not unusual for children to move around even if their family has only gone to the other side of town.

Children are used to comings and goings among their classmates. The chances are a late arrival will be welcomed just like the rest.

And as for the schoolwork, remember that if your child is in some form of pre-school, he'll probably be learning pretty similar things to his contemporaries in class.

The biggest factor in whether your child settles and makes friends is his personality. If he's had no trouble mixing before, it's unlikely that he'll become socially inept just because he starts school a few weeks after many of his classmates.

If you're offered a January start for a young child, consider it with a clear conscience. You may even be given the option of an Easter start date, but bear in mind that a child who starts quite so late into the school year will have only one term before having to get used to a new class, a new teacher and generally a much more intensive workload.

The most important question you have to ask yourself is: do I think my child is mature enough to cope? If the answer is yes, you may well want to go for it. It's your child you're thinking about here, not how much you're going to miss him.

If the answer is no, if all you can foresee is tears, tantrums, and the wriggliest bottom ever to grace the school's assembly, rest assured that school offering late admissions will be more than happy for you to keep him at home just that little bit longer. And if that's what you decide, don't beat yourself up about it. Just enjoy it.

> My daughter has a February birthday. She should have gone to school full-time from the start, but it was too much, too soon. She was crying a lot over nothing, she wasn't sleeping. It wasn't that she wasn't happy at school, she wanted to go, but she was just exhausted. I went down to half-days until Christmas and after that she was fine.
>
> *The mother of a six-year-old*

FIRST DAY

Your child's first day at school is his first life-changing milestone. The day he walked for the first time, the day he said his first words, were both enormous strides forward – but the next day life carried on pretty much as before.

School is different. From the moment he steps into the classroom, your life and his are changed forever. And there's no going back.

From now on, he'll spend about half his waking hours, most days, without you. You can give him the third degree all you like when he comes home, but the fact is that what he does all day from now on will largely be a total mystery to you.

'I've had four children start school and each time it feels like they are being stolen from me,' one mother said.

And that's how it feels for some. For others, it feels like an enormous relief, a chance to grasp back some of the life they feel they've sacrificed and take up their place in what they see as the real world again.

But whether you've been a stay-at-home parent or have worked throughout, sending your child to school for the first time is still one of those emotional moments you'll probably remember forever.

Nothing tugs at the heartstrings quite so much as the sight of your own four-year-old, that baby you brought home from the hospital just a blink ago, all dressed up in his uniform, shoes polished, hair combed, ready for the serious business of school.

Chances are he'll remember this day as long as he lives, just as you remember snippets of your own first day, brought vividly back to life by your mother's frequent recitals of how you howled as you watched her turn her back and leave you for the very first time in the whole of your five years.

Now, of course, the trauma should be so much less. Children are encouraged to visit their schools long before they start.

Many schools send teachers along to nurseries and playgroups to meet their new pupils. Children are generally invited along to a special session in school when they can explore their new classroom and start to feel at home. Some teachers even offer a series of trial mornings to introduce children gradually to what school will be like.

And by far the majority of children starting school will already be well used to waving mum goodbye. Pre-school in all its many guises plays an enormous part in helping a smooth transition to school proper.

But you as parents have to play your part, too. So grit your teeth and put your own emotions aside. This is how to get through that first morning without making your own child cringe as you dissolve in a sea of mascara.

THE WEEK BEFORE

Start sliding those bedtimes forward. The early days at school are exhausting for most children. The last thing they need is late nights. However much routines have slipped during the long summer holidays, now is the time to get back on track. Aim at having them in bed ten minutes earlier every night until they're snuggling down at a time you're happy with. Move the clock forward if you have to. A reassuring routine of cuddling up with a bedtime story will be just what they need to help them get off to sleep in the confusing weeks to come.

THE DAY BEFORE

Talk about school in general terms in the week before they start, but today is probably soon enough for most children to learn that it's school tomorrow. Young children have no real concept of time anyway. Tell them something is ten days away and they haven't a clue what that means. Remember that for them this is something a little bit exciting, a little bit frightening. It isn't Christmas or a trip to Disneyland. This is not the occasion for a countdown chart on the wall. Tell them today that school is tomorrow and they've just enough time to get used to the idea and not quite enough to change their minds about going at all.

Start by drawing a time-line to help them understand what the next day will bring. Four-year-olds told they'll be collected at three have absolutely no grasp of what that means. By 9.30 a.m., they're tugging on the teacher's sleeve asking if it's home time yet.

When you talk to them about what the next day will bring, sit them down and draw a long line across a piece of paper representing their first day at school. Start with a picture of you and them having breakfast, then move along to the time you'll leave home. Draw them halfway through the morning having their drink of milk, enjoying playtime, exploring the toys in the classroom. Then move on to the time when they'll be having lunch, painting, and finally story time. If your child is particularly nervous, talk to the teacher before the holidays about what they'll be doing so that your time-line is as accurate as possible.

Then slip it into your child's pocket for the next day. It will help to reassure them that, however long the line, they will eventually get to that last picture where you're waiting at the gate for them.

THE FIRST MORNING

However chaotic your normal routine, make sure this is the morning you're up in plenty of time to enjoy as quiet and calm a start to the day as it's possible to have with a manic four-year-old tearing around the house.

Try to get at least some breakfast down them, ideally before the uniform goes on. Today's children are scarily used to snacking and it can come as a big shock when a child used to elevenses, tenses, and nineses suddenly finds they're expected to get all the way to lunchtime with a swig of milk if they're lucky to tame the hunger pangs. They may be allowed to take some kind of snack for break time so check in advance. But nothing will substitute for a good breakfast.

Once they're dressed, record the moment with a photograph, give them a hug, and you're off.

TRAVELLING TO SCHOOL

Whatever your work commitments, whatever practicalities will mean for normal days, try to make sure you can go with them to school that first morning at least. Take the day off if you have to. No boss worth his salt could possibly refuse.

If you can, walk. If nothing else, it will burn up some of your child's nervous energy that will otherwise explode into a classroom full of equally excitable four-year-olds. Even if it's too far to walk, it makes sense to get into the habit of parking a ten-minute walk away and doing the rest on foot. Great exercise, and an ideal way to avoid the hell of school-gate congestion.

ARRIVING

Timing here is all. Much as you don't want to be late, arriving too early could be a big mistake. Nothing is guaranteed to scare the pants off a four-year-old quite so much as the sight of a seething playground on the first day back after the summer holidays.

All the older children will be just as hyped-up as the little ones, some will be surprisingly tearful, others will be re-enacting what looks alarmingly like a scene from *Terminator II*. If your child wasn't quaking in his brand-new boots before, he will be now.

So, if school starts at 9 a.m., 8.55 is plenty early enough to put in an appearance. They'll see quite enough of the *Terminator II* brigade at playtime. If you're particularly fortunate, you may be spared much of the first-day, early-morning chaos altogether. Many schools have developed their own system for easing children in. Some, for instance, give each child a different start time for that first morning so that they arrive gradually. Some take only half the class in the mornings and have the other half in the afternoons for the first week or so. And some stagger start dates.

GOING IN

Every teacher will be slightly different in their approach to that first morning, but on one thing they are probably all agreed. Crying children they can cope with, it's wailing mothers that drive them mad.

If ever there was a time for the stiff upper lip, this is it. Walk in with your child, help them hang their coat on their peg, follow the teacher's instructions for what she wants them to do next, then give them a hug and LEAVE.

Don't spend the next ten minutes with your nose pressed to the window waving them the kind of farewell only appropriate for passengers on the *Titanic*.

Don't slip an 'I'm missing you' message into their lunchbox.

Don't park opposite the school gates to see how they cope at playtime.

Get right out of sight and then, if you feel the need, have a good old weep on somebody's shoulder. It's a big moment. You're allowed.

HOME TIME

Allow plenty of time for getting to school, particularly if you're going by car. If you thought the traffic outside school was bad this morning, wait until you see how bad it gets at home time.

However long a day it has seemed to you, remember that it's probably seemed four times as long to the child you sent in at nine o'clock. They might come out all excited, they might tell you every last dot and dash of their day, but the chances aren't high. Ask them what they've been doing, and odds on they'll say: 'Nothing'.

It's best not to press the point. A grilling now is the last thing they need.

Go home and do something familiar and reassuring. Field all those calls from grannies and friends wanting to know how they've got on. Let your child tell you about their day when they're ready.

Then get them to bed early and turn out the light.

Bear in mind the story of the confident four-year-old who sought out his head teacher at the end of the first day.

'Thank you very much,' said the well-mannered child. 'I've had a really lovely time, but I don't think I'll be coming again.'

The harshest lesson your child will have learned today is that they've got it all to do again tomorrow.

JUST FOR DADS

For many mums, the day their child starts school is a life-changing separation. For many dads, life carries on just as before.

When their children go to school, they might have a bit of a lump in their throats on that first morning, but after that not very much changes from their perspective. Most dads leave for work before that hysterical last-minute panic that pervades most households on a school day. And when they come home, their children are generally long back. Life, from a working dad's perspective, must seem pretty much the same as always.

Trust us, it's not. Here are some tips that might just keep you out of the doghouse in those emotionally charged months surrounding your child's start at school.

- Take your partner seriously when she cries all over the school admissions form. Your child's first day at school may still be many months away, but even the routine of filling in the forms will bring the reality of the inevitable home. Be sympathetic. For many mothers, whether they've worked or been stay-at-home mums, sending their children to school is an enormous wrench. And for her this is the first practical step towards it. She won't be the first to smear the form with tears.
- Encourage your partner to make plans for when your child is at school. If she's taken a career break, she's going to need support in adjusting to a very different lifestyle once your children are at school. She'll welcome your support in helping her to plan ahead so

that her days aren't one long, empty drag, waiting for the 3 p.m. home-time bell.

- Making plans for the future doesn't mean lining her up a full-time job from 1 September and bringing her leaflets on pension plans. She might be desperate to go back to her career. Or she might want to think about part-time work, retraining, even a whole new career path. She might want to go back to work full-time or she might not want to go at all. Talk together about all your options. Particularly bear in mind that few jobs, however part-time, stop for the school holidays.

- Underestimate at your peril just how upset your wife may be as all those final hurdles in the run-up to school come along. Your child's last day at playgroup, his trial day at school, that last summer holiday of those long days of freedom – any one of these could reduce your partner to floods of tears. And, as for the day she has to buy the new school uniform, stand by with the Kleenex. Chances are you're going to need them.

- Even if you can't be there for that first day at school, call your partner as soon as she's home. This is a big day for your child. It's a big day for her, too. A call to check on how she's feeling will earn you lots of Brownie points.

AND WHAT ABOUT YOU?

How are you likely to feel about your child starting school? A growing number of dads now play a huge part in raising their children and are very involved in their education. Many do the dreaded taxiing around on the school run. They also tend to be much more pragmatic about sending their children to school.

A lot do feel a pang of sentimentality about their child reaching another milestone. But most take the view that their children are ready for school, that nursery – with all that play dough and painting – wasn't stretching their child enough, that they were ready for something a bit more structured to challenge their intellect.

At the same time, many worry even more than the mother about how their child will cope with the rough and tumble of school life. Dads, who still remember rough and tumbling themselves, worry about how this child – who suddenly seems terribly mollycoddled by mum – will get by when three boisterous five-year-olds jump on his back and start re-enacting their favourite scene from *Power Rangers*.

Many dads have mixed feelings about what school does to their child. Part of them mourns the loss of innocence that comes with mixing with their peers all day. Part of them frets that their sons, in particular, will be picked on for being too innocent because they still haven't plucked up the courage to watch *Monsters Inc.* all the way through.

And, as for their daughters, there probably isn't a dad alive who hasn't recoiled in horror at the sight of their four-year-old singing pop songs and dancing like a teenager. Sadly, that's school for you.

HOW YOU CAN HELP

The most important thing to remember is that, hard as it may be, life for your child and your family has moved on. The start of school is a massive upheaval. Your child is likely to be tired, touchy, moody and not a little confused.

Make time for him. Listen to him read. Chat to him when he's in the bath. Read him bedtime stories. Give him lots of support and reassurance.

And then make yourself a pledge that you'll go on doing that, not just now when it's all new and scary and uncertain, but for the rest of his days at school. You've no idea what a difference it could make.

5 THE EARLY YEARS

So what can you expect from your child's first couple of years in full-time education?

RECEPTION

For both parent and child, that first year in school is a journey into the unknown.

Everything about school is new to the child and just as new and unnerving to the parents. However clued-up we try to be, it's very hard to imagine what day-to-day life will be like for our children. Will it be nursery school by any other name? Or will it be school as we remember it, with rows of desks and a teacher writing spellings on a dusty blackboard?

The answer is that reception classes are a bit of a hybrid. They start out looking remarkably like nursery and during the course of the year transform themselves so that the days become more and more like school.

And the hope is that the children will change, too. Children who arrive with fidgety bottoms and the concentration span of a gnat should slowly evolve over that first year into schoolchildren, raring to go on the starting blocks of that first key stage of the national curriculum.

So, as a parent, what can you expect when you wave your child off to school for the first time with a damp hanky and a chin-up smile? This is what the reception year is likely to hold.

WHAT WILL MY CHILD DO ALL DAY?

Well, most of the time, he'll be playing. In fact, to him, it will probably seem as though he's playing pretty much all the time.

Learning through play is vital for four-year-olds. They enjoy what they're doing and they don't even notice just how much they're learning along the way.

A child who spends half an hour pretending to be a baker, counting out plastic currant buns to his classmates, has in his eyes been playing shop. He's hardly likely to come home and tell you he's been doing maths and role-playing to improve his social skills – even though the teacher might see it that way.

Role-play is very important in helping young children develop. Reception class pupils come to school with a whole mishmash of past experiences. Some will have been to the school's nursery, some will have been to playgroup, some will have gone through day nurseries, and some will never have left their mothers' side. A big part of the reception year is getting all those children to gel and come together as a group, ready for that move up into Year One.

And don't run away with the idea that reception children get off scot-free when it comes to the more formal side of education. From the off, most will be using a phonic-based scheme to learn their letter sounds. Methods vary, but many teachers favour a scheme that links an action to a sound and letter. To teach a child 't', for instance, the whole class might turn their heads from side to side as though they were watching a tennis match, and repeat the sound, 't, t, t,' for tennis.

Children will also increasingly do more writing and those who are ready will start to learn reading skills. Over a period of weeks, they're likely to be given 45 key words to learn, a few at a time, either on separate pieces of paper or on word lists, and will bring them home to practise until they can recognise each one at first glance.

Those key words are among the most commonly used in the English language. They crop up time and again. The aim is that by learning them so thoroughly a child will recognise them at once, so that when it comes to reading books they'll have at least some words in each sentence that they know.

Children will also, of course, begin to learn the basics of maths, so there will be lots of counting, adding, sorting and taking away.

HOW WILL I KNOW HOW MY CHILD IS DOING?

Oh, you'll know. Count your blessings. You'll be kept more informed of your child's progress than even the parents whose children started school a couple of years ago.

Under the new system, each reception child is given a foundation stage profile, which is a booklet recording their achievements. There's a space for the child's photograph on the front and inside is listed in brightly coloured boxes all the things that they might achieve by the end of the year. So, for instance, under the section on language and literacy, there's a box marked, 'Links sounds to letters, naming and sounding letters of the alphabet'. When the child can do that, the teacher will tick the box and indicate in which term the child achieved it.

The parents generally get to see the document during the year and can add their own comments to those of the teacher.

Most schools also hold at least a couple of parents' evenings during the course of the year. The first is generally only weeks into the first term so that parents get an early indication of how their child is settling in.

But if you have any worries or queries about your child's progress, don't wait for a parents' evening that may be months away. Ask to talk to the teacher, ideally at the end of the day by appointment, so that she's not trying to give you her full attention while 25 excitable four-year-olds are just arriving for class.

WHY IS MY RECEPTION-AGE CHILD STUDYING WITH YEAR ONE CHILDREN?

This can happen in some schools. The law in England limits the number of children in infant classes with one qualified teacher to thirty. Some schools keep the number lower by siphoning off some of the reception children – often the older pupils – into a mixed class that also has some Year One children.

Sometimes the children are reunited with their year group when they move into the juniors, but some schools keep mixed classes throughout.

RECEPTION AND PARENTS

The reception year offers you the chance to forge links with the school and your child's teacher that will be stronger than at any other time throughout your child's entire education.

Reception teachers rely on parents not only to support their child's learning, but to turn them into happy, willing pupils. The aim is that the children will feel valued at home and valued in school. That helps them to arrive in school happy, secure and ready to learn.

The door to a good reception class is always open. Parents are encouraged to build a good rapport with that first teacher, a relationship that allows for honesty on both sides.

The parent needs to be able to come to the teacher with anything that might be bothering them or their child, however trivial it may seem. And the teacher needs to be able to say to the parent: 'We had a bit of a problem today ...' without it being a big issue.

The scenario goes something like this. You pick up your child at the school gate and have the usual conversation that revolves around you asking what he did all day and him saying that he can't remember.

Two hours later, they're in the bath and it all comes spilling out. Tears before bedtime.

What on earth, you wonder, can have made them so distressed?

'I went to my usual seat in the hall at lunchtime AND JOHNNY WAS SITTING IN IT!' they wail.

The temptation to say, 'Is that all?' is almost overwhelming. But to this child, *your* child, this has become a problem of monumental proportions. He has worried about it *all* day. And he's worrying now that when he goes for lunch tomorrow, Johnny will be in his seat again, damn him.

To you and the rest of the universe, this is nothing. To him, it's a big thing. This is where that special relationship between you and the reception teacher should come in.

In no other class in the school could you reasonably bring yourself to discuss the thorny issue of the lunchtime seat with your child's teacher. But a good reception teacher will recognise the enormity of the problem.

A child who isn't happy isn't learning. And unhappiness can spring from the most unlikely sources for a child of four.

Obviously, you shouldn't go running to the teacher every time your child has a minor problem in his day, but if something even apparently trivial is causing your child real angst it's worth sorting out.

A good reception teacher won't dismiss a problem that's seriously worrying a child. If you feel your child is struggling to make friends, if you know he hasn't been to the school toilet in a fortnight, talk to the teacher. With a bit of sympathy and a lot of diplomacy, she'll soon have the problem sorted.

WHAT IF MY CHILD WON'T SETTLE?

Oh, what a nightmare. Everybody else's child seems to be trotting happily into school and yours is the one throwing a spectacular paddy at the classroom door.

Finally, they're prised, kicking and screaming, from your grasp and you're expected to trot home and not give it another thought all day. Leaving a child in deep distress is soul-destroying for a parent. It may not last long, but at the time it seems to go on forever.

For some children, that separation from mum is extraordinarily tough. And for some mums, too, it can be heartbreaking. Losing perhaps their youngest or only child to school is genuinely traumatic. They may need as much support in getting through those first few weeks as their child.

The good news for parents faced with tears and tantrums is that almost always the child is milking the situation for all it is worth. Most children who make a scene when mum leaves are down on the carpet playing happily before she's got home. The children are not exactly devious; they're just making a point.

If you have to leave your child in tears, don't let it ruin your day. Ring the school half an hour later, or ask them to ring you. The chances are your child will be ironing away in the home corner and not giving you a second thought.

But what if they're not? What if your child is one of the very few who finds that move to school utterly terrifying? What if he's clinging to you at the school gates, begging you not to send him in? What if he's sobbing his way through every hour of every day? What if he wakes up in the night worrying about the day ahead?

What if he can't enjoy Sundays because Monday is coming and Monday means school?

Well, the first thing you need to do is go to see the teacher without your child and lay your cards on the table. Then, between you, you need to work out a strategy that will appeal to your child and hopefully break the cycle.

Could you, for instance:

- **Set up a simple reward scheme:** The child could have a sticker for every time they arrive at school smiling with some kind of reward to aim for.
- **Use a distraction technique:** Could the teacher give your child a

special job or responsibility to distract him from his distress? Could he fetch the register, put straws in the milk, feed the class hamster?

- **Use your imagination:** One reception teacher, for instance, has a mirror with a smiley face painted on it. If a child is distressed, her classroom assistant gets them to look in the mirror. 'Here,' she says. 'There's a smile waiting just for you. Put it on and we'll go and play.' Problem solved.
- **Ask your child to make something for you during the school day:** He might draw you a picture or make you a card. For some children, it helps to keep that link going with home.
- **Offer your help as a parent volunteer:** Your child may settle better if he sees you as being part of the school. Be warned. This is a risky strategy. It can work, but if your child cries all the more when you leave, don't go back!

If, despite trying every trick in the book, your child still hasn't settled, you need to talk to the teacher again and look at all your options. It may be that a very young child just isn't ready for that day-long wrench from mum. Remember that in any reception class there may be children who were born in the same week, but a year apart. The youngest will have just celebrated their fourth birthday, while the oldest in the class could already be five. Also, children mature at different rates – this can accentuate problems for younger children.

If your four-year-old is really struggling, see if you can work out some kind of compromise. The last thing you want to do is make his life a misery and risk putting him off school for life. Switching to half-days and gradually introducing him to full days may be a better option.

DISCIPLINE AND THE VERY YOUNG CHILD

No matter how hard we try as parents, some children just aren't ready for that leap into all the formalities that come with starting school.

It would be wonderful if we all had well-behaved, well-mannered children we could trust to keep out of mischief all day, but in the real world many children find it virtually impossible to be good for ten minutes at a stretch, never mind six hours.

If you fear that bad behaviour could mar your child's start at school, you may well be worried about how the teacher will react. Clearly, it varies from teacher to teacher, but in many schools, the emphasis on positive discipline starts right from the start.

It works something like this. Say the teacher is trying to take the register and one child starts wandering around the room. Instead of giving the wanderer a severe reprimand, she turns her attention to the children who are behaving.

'Johnny, George, you are sitting nicely. Have a look everyone and see how nicely they are sitting.' With a bit of luck, the wanderer will take the hint and sit down.

In any event, you may well find your worries about how your child will behave are totally unfounded. A child who behaves like a demon at home will often transform into a model pupil for a teacher they want to impress. Just wait until that first parents' evening. You may not recognise the little angel the teacher describes as your own.

In my opinion, the person who knows the child best is the parent. The reception class teacher has to be prepared to listen to the parent and not feel they know everything. There's no place in schools for that 'I've been teaching for so many years and I know everything' attitude. We only have a child for so many hours a day. We can't know them the way their parents do. We have to listen to what the parents say.

Equally, the parent should be prepared to listen to the reception class teacher who has the best interests of their child at heart. Every child has the potential to do well. What they need most at this age is the time and confidence to develop.

A reception class teacher

My child used to cry when I left him. Not at first, but after the Christmas holiday. I think that's when the reality of school, the fact that it would go on and on, first hit him. However upset you are as a parent, you have to stay positive. You have to keep pointing out all the good things about school and reminding them of how much they've learned. We had a reward chart, too, with a sticker for every day he went into school without crying. After so many stickers, he was allowed a new toy.

The mother of a five-year-old

Crying became such a habit that I asked if my little girl could walk to school with a friend one morning to change the pattern. The next day she came with me and she didn't cry. It just broke the cycle.

The mother of a six-year-old

Fun games with maths for reception children

Build a tower: You'll need a dice and some building blocks or Lego bricks. Take turns to roll the dice. Collect the number of bricks shown on the dice and add them to your tower. The first to ten wins.

Roll a shape: Cut out twelve shapes, three each of triangles, squares, rectangles and circles. Take turns to roll a dice and collect a shape that has the same number of sides as the number shown, e.g. throw four and collect a square. The first to have four different shapes wins.

Spot the difference: Draw a row of six big coloured spots. In turn, one player closes their eyes. The other player hides some of the spots with a sheet of paper. The first player looks and says how many spots are hidden. Try the same thing again with a different number of spots.

One more, one less: Take a dice, a coin, and some building blocks or Lego bricks. Take turns to roll the dice. Build a tower with the number of bricks shown, then toss the coin. Heads means take one brick off. Tails means add one on. If you can guess how many bricks there'll be in your tower now, you get to keep them. First to collect twenty wins.

Practise counting: Take a random number under ten and count on from there. Pick a different number and count back to zero. Choose a different starting number each time.

THE LEAP TO YEAR ONE

So, your child has successfully completed the reception year. The early tears have stopped. They're coming home reasonably good-tempered. They had an excellent end-of-year report. Is the worst behind you? Well, sorry, but the honest answer is, not necessarily.

For many children, the move to Year One is a huge leap and an even bigger shock. Where reception was a smooth and gradual transition from playgroup or nursery, there's no disguising that Year One is school proper.

In some schools, once children cross the barrier into Year One, the trappings of childhood are left behind. Gone for many is the Lego, the dolls' house and the home corner, and in their place are word lists and number bonds. It's work, work, work. No wonder the children don't know what's hit them.

So, why the change? And how can you help your child cope?

THE CURRICULUM

Here's the reason why things are so different. Year One is the child's first taste of Key Stage 1 of the national curriculum. That often brings with it a much more formal approach.

A big chunk of the school day is swallowed up by the literacy hour and a daily maths lesson, both intended to drive up standards from the very start of formal education.

The policy means that the whole class works together at the same time for an hour of literacy and around 45 minutes of number work. Because many children have lost their concentration by the time the lunch bell rings, both these key lessons tend to happen in the mornings.

Although all the children are studying the same subject together, they will generally be split into groups to work according to their ability. It may be, for example, that a teaching assistant will be hearing one group read while the teacher helps the rest of the class with a writing exercise. The more able children might fill a page with news of what they did at the weekend, writing with a pencil on a plain piece of paper with a line guide underneath. The less able might have a photocopied sheet giving them words and guidance to help them structure their work.

They might then have playtime and come back to a maths lesson. That could be addition, subtraction, graphs, shapes, measuring or telling the time.

Now you know why they're shattered by home time.

WHAT ABOUT THE REST OF THE DAY?

Schools vary in what they do with the rest of the day. Some continue to have more formal lessons for at least some of the afternoons. They might, for instance, work on that term's topic learning about a subject such as dinosaurs or the Victorians. They'll probably do some science, art, music, PE and technology (working with computers).

Many schools stick to a structured timetable, with little or no time allocated to children for playing or choosing their own activities. Others incorporate play as an important part of the curriculum and value it in its own right. They see it as an important boost to developing children's social skills, imagination and creativity.

Even some of the schools which have favoured the no-toys approach are now rethinking their policy and putting an element of play back into the school day for Year One children, who are still only the same age as most of their parents were when they first went to school.

Some teachers found that making such young children work all day was counterproductive. The children, particularly the less academically gifted, were simply unable to cope. Instead of learning at a tremendous pace, they were actually getting nowhere. By putting play back into their days, the children coped better and learned faster. And were doubtless a lot happier into the bargain.

HOW DO THE CHILDREN ADAPT?

Most do – some love the formal approach and knowing exactly what's expected of them. Others don't. For a lot of children, the change to a much more formal education is just too drastic. They're upset, tearful and tired.

As a parent, you need to be prepared for a tough countdown to that first half-term. Keep your child motivated by rewarding him for his efforts, not necessarily a material reward, but lots of praise for what he's achieved. He will be learning at a breathtaking pace, expected to grasp all those basic new skills that he needs before he can move on. And he's doing it all – maths, reading, writing – all intensively, all at the same time.

For some, it's just too much, too soon. You should expect your child to be tired, but if you feel that it's going beyond that, that he is being pushed too far, don't hesitate to talk to his teacher.

Tell her what things are like at home, and ask for her guidance in striking a better balance between what's ideal and what's achievable. And if there are problems, don't ignore them. If your child comes home so completely exhausted that you feel it's unreasonable to bring out the homework books, don't just leave it and let him face the music. Talk to the teacher about what happened. Most teachers will understand and will work with you to help your child cope.

THE BENEFITS

For some Year One *is* all work and no play. For others, it's a baptism of fire. But it's not all bad.

As a parent, stand back in amazement and watch your child fly. Most children achieve remarkable things during this school year. If you thought the progress in reception was impressive, Year One is often the time when for many children it all starts to click into place.

Children who were struggling to put a couple of sentences together at the start of the year might leave the class able to write their own stories. Handwriting that was once the size of a house becomes clear, neat and legible. Numbers start to mean something. The children can do impressive sums, they can tell the time.

So, yes, the going may be tough, but take heart. It's quite possible that for some, it will never be quite so tough again.

I have twins who were split into different classes at the end of the reception year. I was gutted. My little girl became introverted, quiet, her sleep pattern was completely different, she wouldn't communicate, she wouldn't come near me for cuddles.

She said she had no one to play with, so I used to go and sit outside the playground at lunchtimes to see how she was getting on. I thought it couldn't possibly be as bad as she said it was, but actually when I saw it for myself it was.

Then she was invited out to tea with some of her new classmates and I invited them back to us. Before long, she had lots of new friends. After the first term, she was completely back to normal.

And, without his sister mothering him, her brother blossomed. His school work improved and he really matured.

The mother of eight-year-old twins

---

6 HOW YOUR CHILD COULD CHANGE

It's nine o'clock in the morning. You've had a long chat over breakfast, your child has skipped to school, the bell rings and he turns to give you a big farewell hug.

'See you later,' he says. And in he runs, happy as Larry.

The clock ticks forward. It's 3 p.m. The house has been deathly quiet all day. You can't wait to collect him and hear his news.

The classroom door opens and out he comes, the three o'clock monster. The happy-go-lucky child you sent in has turned into a beast.

'Good day?' you ask, tentatively.

'No,' he snaps.

'Oh, dear, are you a bit tired?'

'No.'

'Shall we catch the bus?'

'No!'

Oh, joy. This is the downside of school, familiar to thousands of parents who come to dread the home-time bell. They send one child in at the beginning of the day and at the end a different child emerges with the face of a gargoyle and the personality of Satan.

He is stubborn, argumentative and aggressive. You send him to his room and he won't go. You cook him his favourite tea and suddenly he wants fish fingers instead.

He won't do his homework, he won't play with his sister, he does unspeakable things to the cat.

And he cries all the time. He pricks a finger and lets out a scream fit to earn him a starring role in *Casualty*. He knocks the marbles down in Kerplunk and the house reverberates to yells of 'It's not fair! It's not fair! It's not fair!'

You don't recognise him any more. It feels like your child has turned into the world's first four-year-old adolescent and you'll never get him back.

And then suddenly it's the weekend and gargoyle boy disappears to be replaced by your own sweet-natured child again.

'School!' you mutter under your breath. 'Don't you just love it?'

What makes it worse for those of us whose children turn into monsters is that many children don't. They are the ones who spring out of school clutching pictures bearing 'I love you, Mummy' messages. They skip past your scowling horror with a chirpy: 'Bye, Charlie!' and then they're off to bake cookies or visit ailing grandparents or deliver charity envelopes or whatever else you, in your current state of vitriol, imagine they do with their evenings.

If they can come out of school like that, what's wrong with your child? Is he mixing with the wrong crowd? Is he being bullied? Is he – worst-case scenario – misbehaving in class?

Relax – the chances are that he's none of these. Any teacher will tell you that children who uncharacteristically start misbehaving at home at the end of a busy school day are generally angels in class. More often than not, they're the ones who concentrate on their work, sit bolt upright in assembly, are polite, well-mannered, and wouldn't say boo to the proverbial goose.

After all that exemplary behaviour, it's hardly surprising that they're tired and need to let off steam at the end of the day. Nor is it particularly surprising that they should want to experiment with some of the bad behaviour they see in school. Cockiness, aggression, defiance – sadly, they'll encounter it all at some stage, no matter which school you choose.

Knowing why it happens hardly makes it any easier to handle. Much as you might try to sympathise, the fact remains that, unless you get a grip, that unacceptable behaviour your child sees in school will seep into your home life. Before you know it, the transformation into a teatime monster will have become a habit that's hard to break.

Have a quiet word with the teacher without your child. Tell them how worried you are and ask what his behaviour is like at school.

If the teacher has no worries, this is a time for firmness. Deep breath. This is how it's done.

Taming the three o'clock monster:

1. Accept that a young child who has been cooped up all day, expected to behave and told to concentrate, is quite likely to go wild when they come out of school. In summer, it's a good idea to go home via the park. It certainly makes sense to walk at least part of the way home and burn off some of that excess energy.
2. If safety isn't a problem, if your child isn't doing anything likely to endanger him or anyone else, bad behaviour is best ignored.
3. Use distraction techniques. Just as he's about to throw his most spectacular wobbly, change the subject completely. Tell him anything he's not expecting – that *Robot Wars* is launching a new competition, that there's an enormous crane at the bottom of your street, that his Granny has got a new budgie – anything that might get him thinking of something else. Or try: 'Come on, let's go and do this instead.' It might work.
4. If the behaviour is bad to the point of being dangerous or socially unacceptable, you have to act. You can start with: 'Please stop doing that.' Then: 'I've told you once, please stop doing that.' Then: 'That's it. Go to your room [or whatever your particular sanction is].' Then: 'GO TO YOUR ROOM!' And you have to mean it. If they won't go, take them there. There's being cheeky and there's going too far. Once a child becomes truly defiant, you have to act.
5. Don't be too hard on yourself if you do lose your cool. A child of even the most laid-back parent knows how to press all the buttons until eventually their parent loses their temper. Everybody does it sometimes.

So how do you stop yourself getting into that situation in the first place? The important thing to remember is that young children like routines. Going to school is a major upheaval for them. No wonder their behaviour often goes off the boil.

But no child likes to be out of control. That's just not the way children were designed to be. They like sensible limits and they like to know where they stand. Parents may sympathise with their tiredness, but are doing them no favours if they let the behaviour get out of control.

If bad behaviour becomes a habit with your child – and one that's guaranteed to win them 100% of your attention – he'll keep on doing it. Even having you cross with him is better than being ignored.

Not only do you need to reward good behaviour, you need to manipulate it. Take that tired child home and do absolutely nothing together.

Consciously make an effort to have some time in the week when you do nothing. Just cuddle up on the settee and enjoy each other's company.

Entertaining your child, being there for him, doesn't mean you always have to be doing something. Doing nothing is fine sometimes. So is watching a bit of television, making a mess together, doing something really boring that he wants to do.

And if he wants to play with toys you thought he'd grown out of, fine. Remember that he's going through that awful dilemma at school – am I ready for this or am I not – it's not uncommon for children to regress.

Some wet the bed. Some even start to use baby talk. Deeply annoying as this is for parents whose child always talked clearly from his first utterance, it's just another symptom of massive change.

Get cross about it, turn it into a battleground, and he'll do it all the more, because it gets your attention and that's what it's all about.

As parents, the best thing you can do is go back to that earlier stage of development with him. Give him lots of kisses and cuddles. Make him feel safe and secure enough to move on – and he will.

> If your child comes home exhausted, sit down and have a cuddle. Don't do anything, just sit there and be quiet with them. That's probably the single nicest thing you can do – just be with someone just because they are them.
>
> *A child psychiatrist*
>
> My children were uncontrollable when they came out of school. I think they found it quite restricting. It took a while to get them into the routine, particularly after the Christmas holiday.
>
> *The mother of six-year-old twins*

> **TOP TIP:** Many of today's young children are scarily used to snacking. Going to school, with its rigid regime of when you can and can't eat, comes as a tremendous shock. Children come out of school ravenous and hunger alone accounts for a lot of the home-time tantrums. Take a snack with you, but capitalise on this precious time. So hungry are they that they'll probably eat just about anything. This is no time for crisps, chocolate and coke. Take healthy snacks, fruit, and fruit-juice cartons. They'll be so hungry, they might not even notice the goodness going in.

GROWING UP

One thing you can be sure of when you send your child to school – big change is on the way.

Unless you are remarkably blessed, the fact that your child will be spending most of their waking hours with other children and away from you is bound to change them.

In this new and complex social world in which they're expected to carve their own niche, all kinds of influences, both good and bad, creep in.

They'll have to learn to rub along with other children who have their own ideas and values. And the way those children think and behave will be largely influenced by the ideas and values of their parents. Is it any wonder that sometimes you'll feel you hardly know your own child any more?

So, what can you expect? Well, here are just some of the things you might find sneaking home from school.

For girls:

- **A touch of the teenage tinies:** That little girl you sent into school in her white ankle socks will be wanting hipster jeans and T-shirts emblazoned with 'Babe' before you know it. She'll want the Cheeky Girls on in the car and will soon know all the actions to a song with the immortal lyrics: 'McDonalds, McDonalds, Kentucky Fried Chicken and a Pizza Hut'. We kid you not. And she'll go to parties where the five-year-olds look fifteen and come home with party bags full of lip gloss and hair glitter.
- **Brazen cheek:** She'll push her luck with that eye rolling, arms folded, 'whatever' attitude you thought you'd escape until the onslaught was at least hormonally charged.
- **Blackmail:** She'll have you thinking you're the worst mother in the world. 'But *everybody* else is allowed ...'
- **Maturity:** Well, it couldn't be *all* bad news. Little girls might grow up frighteningly fast, but they can be lovely with it. They often love reading and writing. They leave letters for the fairies at the bottom of the garden. They write and perform their own plays. They keep a diary. They bring pictures home from school that say 'I missed you, Mummy' on the bottom. They bring friends home for tea who *don't* wreck their room and *do* say thank you.

Boys, on the other hand:

- **Become incredibly silly:** They laugh uproariously at each other's jokes, whether or not they have any hint of a punch line. They find anything to do with wee, poo, or bottoms hilarious. At least they outgrow that in time. Sadly, anything to do with breaking wind can often remain hilarious to them for the rest of their natural lives.

- **Turn hyper-competitive:** With only minimum adult intervention during those long spells in the playground, instinct takes over. They are back in the jungle, learning how to survive. They pounce on each other like tiger cubs learning how to fight. Life becomes one long battle for supremacy whether it's who can run fastest, who's the best at computer games, who owns the best Beyblade, who wins at Top Trumps. If only there was some way of circumnavigating nature and explaining that the days when you had to be a psychopath to survive are long gone. Even the leader of the pack will probably end up in a nine-to-five office job one day.
- **Become boisterous and noisy:** Invite more than one at a time to tea and you're a saint. We give it half an hour before one of them thinks what a wheeze it would be to throw a teddy at the lampshade. Regain control if you can.
- **Stay children longer:** However wearing boys can be, the chances of them taking an interest in the Cheeky Girls before puberty are reassuringly slim.

Remember, too, that the new influences your child faces at school might come as a shock to you, but are probably just as much of a shock to him. You can't stop him growing up, but he's still your child. Your influence, your outlook, your rules, still matter far more than you might think.

MAKING THE MOST OF TIME WITH A YOUNGER CHILD

The time you spend with your child becomes doubly precious once he is at school. The secret is to enjoy it without falling into the trap of trying to cram so much in that he can't possibly keep up.

School brings with it a whole new social life and a whirlpool of opportunities. Snap them all up and don't be surprised when your child explodes in a foot-stamping, door-slamming, toy-throwing bout of hysteria. Overprotect him by turning all the invitations down and you could find your child frozen out of a social circle still organised and run by eager mums.

It's a difficult balancing act and how much children do out of school should depend largely on their personality. If they have the stamina of a wildebeest and the patience of Mother Teresa then, yes, they might manage two parties, a tea invitation, gymnastics and swimming all in the same week.

If, on the other hand, they're likely to be so exhausted by the second party that there's a serious risk of them causing an embarrassing scuffle in musical chairs, it might make more sense to turn something down.

And it certainly makes sense to think long and hard before cramming every night of the week with organised activities. Young children driven on a relentless timetable from Rainbows to piano lessons to junior tennis to ballet must be exhausted. There's a real danger that in the end all they'll really enjoy are the conversations they had with mum in the car en route from one activity to the next.

Never underestimate the value of the time your child spends at home with you. For all schoolchildren of all ages and abilities, a day in the classroom should be a challenge. The teacher's job is to stretch them. They're tired when they come out. They're supposed to be. And, like all of us after a hard day at the office, sometimes children just want to come home and relax.

The time you spend with your child is also a big investment in his learning. It isn't only when you're poring over the homework books that you're helping with his education. Just enjoying yourselves together is a great way to boost his confidence and self-esteem.

Family time is hugely important to children. It's the time when they get to ask questions, talk about anything that might be worrying them, and have some fun. It's also immensely reassuring to an older child expected to spend all day at school while mum is at home with a younger sibling.

That doesn't mean that for parents trying to juggle work and home commitments, finding family time has to be yet another thing to beat yourself up about. Family time can be something as simple as sitting round the table enjoying a meal together. Turn the TV off and talk to each other. However much they create when the TV goes off, all children revel in a conversation that revolves around them.

Anything you can do to take the strain off the hectic teatime hour will help. A young child might have less than four hours between leaving school and going to bed. Try to limit how much of that time is eaten up by life's essentials. If you can prepare the meal before your child comes home, you'll have more time to spend with him. Even a zonk in front of the TV for a while is nicer with mum beside you.

And don't stick rigidly by old routines that get in the way of busy school days. Does your child really need a bath *every* night? Forget it some nights and have a game instead.

Try to squeeze in some of the activities your child loved when the days were long and uncluttered. Stick things, make things, draw things, play with his favourite toys, kick a football in the garden.

Dig out the family photo albums, watch some old family videos, talk about your child and his place in your family. Make him feel special.

And make a conscious effort to get as much as you can out of the weekends without feeling the need to fill every spare minute. Even the most energetic party animal might surprise you by turning into a home bird once he's out at school all week.

It isn't so much what you do that counts. The important thing is that you're doing it *together*, reinforcing the message that, while your child might be out at school all day, his role in the family is just as important as it always was.

So, yes, all the time you're together he's learning communication skills and picking up more knowledge about the world, but the crucial thing is the confidence building, the self-esteem that comes with feeling secure. That's the key.

7 DISCIPLINE

When it comes to discipline, parents tend to fall into two camps. Half think that any school is far too strict, the children too regimented, the discipline too controlling. The other half think that things have gone to the dogs since they were at school and would happily see the return of the slipper.

The children often favour a strict approach. Strange as it might seem, they are generally much more settled with a teacher who sets high standards and won't allow children to waver from them.

Whether at home or at school, children like to know the boundaries. They feel more secure in a setting where the way they are expected to behave is clearly defined. And they certainly want to know that the teacher has got the measure of the naughty kids. You don't have to be a telltale to rejoice when the teacher spots Horrid Harry turning his maths worksheet into a paper aeroplane and keeps him in all playtime.

It's human nature to want bad behaviour to be found out and punished. Adults are no different. How many parents like a boss who lets the skivers get away with murder? How much does a boss rise in our estimation when the colleague who has spent half the day gossiping in the toilets is landed with a towering pile of files at five o'clock on a Friday afternoon?

By the same token, adults and children alike, no one loves a bully. For discipline to be effective, a teacher has to be firm but fair. It's her only chance of keeping order over thirty-odd children while still retaining their respect.

There's a saying in teaching: 'Never smile before Christmas.' What it means is that if you let the discipline slip too early, you've lost them.

In practice, you'll be pleased to know that most teachers allow themselves the occasional smile before then, but the majority certainly start out much firmer with a new class than they'll be later in the year.

Unless they've got the discipline established within the first three or four weeks, they know they're sunk and it will be an uphill battle for the rest of the year.

Expect your child's new teacher to be dogmatic about rules, at the beginning at least. What she's doing is setting the boundaries so that children know just how far they can go. So don't be too disheartened when your child comes home in September with a familiar tale of woe. 'I don't like Mrs Briggs. She's not nearly as nice as my last teacher.' Give it a couple of months and Mrs Briggs could well turn out to be the best thing since sliced bread.

HOW DO SCHOOLS DEAL WITH BAD BEHAVIOUR?

One of the biggest concerns among parents when their child first goes to school is that, without a parent in the role of referee, their child will either be picked on or will misbehave himself.

They read horror stories in the press about children turning up at school with knives, violence in the classrooms, bad language, bullying, and their stomachs churn at the thought of how their youngster will survive.

In reality, in most schools discipline is not a major problem. How schools manage that is a source of wonder. They are somehow expected to be a beacon of desirable behaviour in a society riddled with social problems. They are expected to cope with disruptive children who not so long ago would have gone to special schools designed to cope with their behavioural difficulties. They have to manage all of that without laying so much as a finger on a child. And should, heaven forbid, any of the staff ever lose their temper in the process, as parents do a zillion times, they risk being hauled before the courts and, at worst, being jailed. Scary stuff.

So, just how do they do it? You or I might remember the days of rule by fear, but many schools now opt for a much more subtle approach. Policies on discipline obviously vary from school to school, but it is now common practice to favour a much more positive attitude to get the children on board.

When most parents talk about discipline, what they mean is punishment, but to schools they are not one and the same. To them, discipline isn't about waiting until Horrid Harry thumps someone in the dinner queue; it's about stopping him doing it in the first place.

That means creating an atmosphere in which good manners, politeness and respect for others aren't just something the teachers would like to see, they're something they expect. The school rules don't say: 'You will not do this, you will not do that.' They say: 'This is how we behave in this school, and this is how we expect *you* to behave,' with the emphasis on what teachers want to see, not what they don't.

It's the difference between self-discipline and control. A strict, old-school teacher, very sharp, very severe, very precise, may seem to have perfect control over her class until the moment she's called away. With the control gone, the children are flicking paper pellets at each other, drawing doodles on their neighbour's work, chasing round the classroom like lunatics and leaving drawing pins on her seat.

They behave when the teacher is there, but only out of fear, not out of any sense of right or wrong. When the fear disappears, they're back to the nightmarish children we almost certainly were at their age. And who would want that for their own child?

Parents will recognise the pattern only too well, if not in their own families then in others. Harsh disciplinarian dad rules with a rod of iron, the children are impeccably behaved, then he walks out of the door and the kids run rings round mum. Unless dad plans to spend the rest of his life welded to his children, discipline by fear is a recipe for long-term disaster.

Increasingly, school policy on discipline is that the staff want the children to understand *why* they are expected to behave in a certain way and why other behaviour is unacceptable.

Horrid Harry can expect to spend a lot of time in the head teacher's office, not being punished in the way most of us would consider a punishment, but being made to see the error of his ways. 'When you called that little girl "Fatty", she was really hurt,' the head might say. 'You mustn't do that. I wouldn't like it if it was happening to you.'

You'll be pleased to hear that the reprimand rises according to the scale of the crime. A child who normally behaves well may be easily reduced to tears by a shake of the head and a mild rebuke. 'I can't believe you behaved like this. I'm so disappointed in you. If this happens again ...' often does the trick.

Where children are being routinely aggressive, the head might well rise to the occasion and deliver the mother and father of all tellings off. He might shame them in front of their peers to reinforce the message.

This has the added benefit of letting the well-behaved children know that exceptionally bad behaviour will be stamped out.

At the same time, schools work hard at drumming home the message that good behaviour will be rewarded. Whether it's the winning of a cup or medal, or something as simple as a smiley-face sticker on a sweat-shirt, it all has the same effect. The child feels pleased with himself, he walks out of school and mum is delighted, his self-esteem rises, and he wants more of the same.

It's good behaviour by negotiation and co-operation. And it's life-changing stuff.

> It's all about positive discipline. The phrase is, 'Catch a child being good.'
>
> *A Year Six teacher*

WHEN THINGS GO WRONG

This all sounds idyllic, of course, until yours is the child in bother. All but the most realistic parents go into school imagining their child in the role of victim, not perpetrator.

If your child has behaved badly enough to warrant a visit to the head, you won't necessarily be informed. A head may take the view that in the less serious cases where a child has been reprimanded by him, the incident has been dealt with and that should be the end of the matter.

At other times, he may feel that an incident was serious enough to warrant a call home. He may even ask you to go along for a formal appointment to discuss your child's behaviour.

In some instances, the call may come from you. If you are becoming increasingly worried about some aspect of your child's behaviour, it makes sense to talk to his teacher or even the head. Many behaviour problems can be resolved quite quickly if they are caught early enough.

The important thing is not to panic. Blessed indeed is the parent who gets their child through the entire school system without them once being on the receiving end of a reprimand.

Any meeting about your child's behaviour is bound to stir the emotions. Whether your natural instinct is to go in and defend your child to the hilt or to cringe, scarlet of cheek, in a corner, it makes sense to go well prepared and try to keep calm.

Take some notes with you if you think you're likely to forget what you want to say. Go with someone, ideally your partner or another relative or friend, if you think it will help.

Try to say your piece in a measured way so that the whole thing doesn't dissolve into accusations or tears. The school is far more likely to see your point of view if you put it across calmly and give the head all the information he needs to see a full picture.

If you explain, for instance, that your child has been teased relentlessly by the child he eventually thumped, the school won't condone it, but will understand that he is not the only villain of the piece. It can then work hard with both children to resolve their differences.

If there are problems at home, such as marital break-up or a bereavement that might explain why your child has suddenly gone off the rails, put the school in the picture. Rest assured that the staff will be discreet and treat the information sensitively. But they can't help if they don't know.

As well as having your say, go prepared to listen. However uncomfortable you are with what you're hearing, try not to be too defensive. Ask for specific examples of when and how your child has misbehaved.

Then, crucially, work out a way forward. You need to leave that meeting with some practical steps that might help to prevent problems in the future.

It might be something as simple as agreeing to your child sitting away from his friends. He may be able to move to another class. Whatever you agree, it's important that you and the school decide on the way forward and support each other in its implementation.

Then you need to go home and have a long serious talk with your child. If ever you're going to tear a strip off him, this could well be the time. You might also want to hand out some punishments, something that will hurt far more than a clip round the ear. Ban him from taking part in that important football match, confiscate his Game Boy, have a 'no television' rule for a week.

But whatever you do, the most important thing is to talk. Find out why he's in trouble. Get him to talk about what he thinks of his own behaviour. Explain the changes you've agreed at school. Tell him how disappointed you are, how surprised you are by his behaviour. Promise him your full support in sorting out his problems.

Then agree a way forward for home and school. If his behaviour improves, some of his privileges return.

His self-esteem is probably now at rock bottom. As he improves, start to build it up. Make an issue of it when he helps without being asked, show an interest when he's trying hard with his homework, give him as much of your time as you can, and see the difference.

Keep the school informed about what's happening at home and make sure they communicate with you. If there is an improvement, make sure you praise him for it, and ask his teacher to do the same. Stress the positive.

It might be hard work, it might take weeks, but the benefits could last for years.

BULLYING

Bullying is probably the thing most parents dread when they send their child off to school. And understandably so.

Bullying is nasty, dangerous, and in some cases scars for life. Some of the parents who dread it most will themselves remember the panic, the clammy fear that blighted their own schooldays because a bully's behaviour went unchecked.

Now, schools have anti-bullying policies and children should be safer. Sadly, all too often, bullying happens in secret when adult backs are turned and that makes it still one of the toughest areas for schools to tackle. Parents need to know the warning signs and make sure their children are not suffering alone.

The first thing to remember about bullying is that it's a term much mis-used. People bandy the word about so often and so inappropriately that when true bullying comes along, it's not always taken as seriously as it should be. It's like the colleague who says she's got the flu and takes a week off every time she gets a sniffle. When she does actually catch the flu, nobody believes her.

If two children who were friends yesterday have a one-off fall-out in the playground and one thumps the other then, unacceptable as it is, it's not bullying. If two friends decide to exclude a third and no one talks to her for the whole lunch hour, she may come home heartbroken, but she's not being bullied either.

Bullying is usually something that gets a grip and won't let go. It might never become as physical as that isolated thump in the playground, but its effects can be far worse.

It's often repeated over a period of time, a drip, drip, drip, undermining a child's confidence and self-esteem.

In primary schools, the victim is often someone who is different from everyone else in some way. For whatever reason, they are spotted, isolated, and mercilessly picked on.

And it's not just a problem with boys. Girls are no better. Half of all bullies are female. Usually, boys are bullied by boys, but girls can be bullied by both girls and boys.

And what do the bullies do? Most of their bullying falls into three main categories:

- **Physical:** Things like hitting, kicking, biting, stealing from their victim
- **Verbal:** Shouting names and insults, not once, but over and over again until the victim feels there's no escape
- **Indirect:** Excluding another pupil from the inner circle, not talking to them and encouraging others to follow suit, spreading malicious gossip about them

To a greater or lesser degree, it happens everywhere at some time, in primary school, secondary school, university, the office, etc.

But staff in primary schools, where up to three-quarters of bullying happens in the playground, have a unique problem. They are often dealing with children too immature to know the difference between a row and true bullying. So they get a child of six pointing the finger at another boy and saying, 'He's bullying me,' when what really happened was that the other child stole his place in the lunch queue. If only genuine bullying were so easy to spot and so simple to deal with.

> Parents are too quick to use the term 'bullying', but when your child comes home and says, 'Nobody wants to play with me,' you can't help but feel for them.
> *The parent of a six-year-old girl*

AS A PARENT, HOW DO I PROTECT MY CHILD?

The first thing is to get the fear into perspective. Yes, bullying does happen, but it isn't rife.

It's another of those tricky judgment calls when your child comes home from school in tears. Do you go and see the teacher and risk being thought overprotective? Or do you leave your child to get on with it and risk not supporting him when he needs you most?

Well, here are some of the signs that should set warning bells ringing:

- **Moodiness:** Not a one-off paddy, but behaviour you know is completely out of character
- **Poor work:** A sudden and unexpected deterioration in the work your child does in class
- **Truancy:** Or a desperate reluctance to go to school
- **Health problems:** Such as headaches, stomach aches, anxiety, depression and loneliness

Your child is not necessarily being bullied, but clearly something is going very wrong. See if you can get him to talk and then make an appointment to see his teacher without him.

Don't wait too long. If a child is unhappy at school for any reason, the teacher needs to know. If bullying is the cause, she needs to know without delay.

Don't wait until you're angry. True bullying isn't going to sort itself out. It's totally unacceptable. Your child needs help and he needs it fast.

Talk to him calmly about what has happened. Make notes about specific incidents and then report what you know to his teacher. Be clear on what action the school plans to take, and keep in touch with the school to let them know whether things have improved or whether the problems are continuing.

Remember, however much your child begs and pleads, however fearful he is that shopping the bully will make it worse, you need to get the school involved. No child – and no primary-age child in particular – should ever be left to suffer in silence.

WHAT MAKES A BULLY?

There must be only one thing worse than finding your child is being bullied and that's discovering that your child *is* a bully.

Children who bully others can come from any kind of family and from any background. Many children do it at some time in their lives, sometimes because they've got problems and are acting out aggressive feelings, sometimes because their friends are encouraging them to bully.

They might not know it's wrong, they might be copying the behaviour of someone else in the family they admire, or they may simply know of no better way to mix with their peers.

If you find out your child has been bullying others, you need to explain why it's unacceptable. You also need to ask yourself where the problem stems from and how you can change your child's behaviour.

Don't be afraid to take your problem to the school and ask for help and support. They'll admire your attitude in tackling the problem head-on and will help you stamp it out.

WHAT MAKES A VICTIM?

Children are bullied for all kinds of reasons, but some factors increase the risk. These include:

- Shyness
- Overprotective families
- Belonging to a different racial or ethnic group to the majority
- Having special educational needs or a disability
- Lack of social skills, such as the child who others see as a nuisance

HOW DO SCHOOLS DEAL WITH BULLIES?

The favoured route is prevention as much as cure. Children are encouraged to talk openly about the issue. As part of their studies, they look at why children bully each other and what schools can do to stop it. Victims say they are less worried and more likely to tell someone after studying the topic in class.

The way bullies are dealt with varies from school to school, but the general attitude is that suspected bullying must never be ignored. The teacher or head will generally listen to all the children involved and then lay down action designed to stop the problem. They should then follow up repeatedly to make sure the bullying doesn't flare up again.

In the most serious and persistent cases, particularly involving violence, pupils can be permanently excluded.

8 HOW TO BEHAVE IN SCHOOL: A GUIDE FOR PARENTS

It's not just the children who need a few rules on behaviour. Parents sometimes could do with some guidance themselves.

THE GREEN-EYED MONSTER

Most caring parents start their child at school working on the same theory. 'I'm not bothered about him being top of the class,' they say. 'The main thing is that he's happy in school. As long as he tries hard, as long as he makes friends and behaves himself, that's all that matters.'

For most of us, that lasts about a week. Then we hear that the teacher has been looking at his work and that first niggle of doubt creeps in. What if he isn't up to scratch? What will they think if he spelled his name wrong? What – oh, here we go – if the other children are better than him?

And so it starts. No matter how laid-back we thought we were, no matter how much we vowed we'd never compare our child with someone else's, there's something inbred in most of us which means we just can't help ourselves.

Suddenly, it isn't just how well our own child is doing that's important to us, it's how well he's doing compared to the rest of the class.

You see another child's reading book and you wonder how come he's on Book 6 while your child is still ploughing through the hugely exciting tale of what Roger Red Hat did in Book 5b. And then, shame on you, you start asking questions you know you shouldn't ask.

'Who's in your reading group, Charlie?' you say. 'Who do you sit with for maths?'

Can he remember? Probably not, so then you start to worry that his memory skills aren't up to scratch.

Panic leads you to ask the most probing question of all. Does he ever sit with Katie Burton? Every class has a Katie Burton. Katie is the immaculately behaved child who has been reading fluently since she was three, knew her five times table at four, and has a wall full of gymnastics certificates, which she framed herself.

Is Charlie in her reading group, by any chance?

'No.'

For maths, perhaps?

'No.'

At this innocent early stage, your child has absolutely no idea why the sudden interest in Katie Burton. One of the big advantages of grouping young children according to ability is that generally they remain oblivious to their own shortcomings. Put four children at the same stage of reading together and they assume everyone reads like that. The fact that Katie Burton spends her spare time solo reading *The Lion, the Witch and the Wardrobe* and doing SATs maths papers for fun is something totally beyond their experience.

And, anyway, why would they care? If they're going to compete at something really important, what's wrong with Beyblades?

But you? Oh, you care more than you would ever want anyone to know. One mother, who had laughed uproariously at the school induction day when the head teacher had warned against the perils of jealousy, found herself the worst offender.

'I invited a child back for tea and then sneaked a look in his school bag to see if his reading book was ahead of ours,' she said. 'How bad is that?'

Well, very bad, actually, but hardly unique. Which of us hasn't scrutinised our child's birthday and Christmas cards to see if other children in the class can write better than our own?

But if you're appalled at your attitude to school work, wait until the reward schemes start. Children, on the whole, respond pretty well to reward schemes. Many parents can't handle them at all.

The way it seems to work is this. Lots of schools run some kind of merit system, rewarding children for good behaviour. There's often something like a medal or cup, awarded weekly to a child in assembly in recognition of outstanding effort.

The first week, it tends to go to a child who has worked particularly hard, the Katie Burton of the class, perhaps, who can take it home and squeeze it on to the mantelpiece among her various gymnastics trophies.

In week two, the winner is generally one of the less able children who has impressed the teacher by trying hard.

'That's nice,' you say. 'I'm glad it's gone to someone like that.'

Around week six, the naughtiest boy in the class gets it for not biting anyone that week. To your child, who hasn't bitten anyone since he was two, this must seem a particularly dodgy reason for winning an award, but what does he care? Within thirty seconds of it being handed out, it was playtime and the whole thing was forgotten. But you? You're starting to have your doubts.

It's now week seven and your mantelpiece is still trophy-less. 'Who got the prize this week?' you ask with just a hint of desperation.

'Don't know,' he says.

'You must know!'

'I think it was Emily Parkin.'

Emily Parkin! The little madam you remember from playgroup who was always telling tales.

The naughtiest boy in the class has been singled out for praise, the bossiest girl, so what does this say about where your child stands?

The answer is probably exactly where you'd want him. The chances are he's quietly getting on with his work and behaving himself. His turn to shine will come, it just might not be yet.

The golden rule is to forget the reward scheme, ignore other children's reading books, and don't undermine your child's self-esteem. If you think he's doing well, tell him so. If you think he's earned a reward, do something special as a treat.

Remember your own words: 'As long as he's happy, as long as he's trying.' No one's pretending it's easy, but build up his self-confidence and you might find you need a space on the mantelpiece after all.

WHY THE JEALOUSY?

Don't be too hard on yourself. It's probably not jealousy at all. Nor is it likely to be a sudden burst of late-onset competitive spirit.

Far more plausible is that we send our children to school still weighed down by all the insecurities that dogged our own schooldays.

However blasé we are on day one, when after four weeks our child still hasn't got his first word list, we start to take it all very personally. It isn't his shortcomings that bother us, it's our own.

Are we bad parents? Did we spend rather too much time with the *Fimbles* and not enough with Mick Inkpen? Are we bright enough for the job? Will the teacher be judging us by how much our children know?

The more insecure we become, the more the silly things get to us. Why has that child got a sticker on his sweatshirt and not ours? Why is our neighbour's child in a different reading group? And where the hell is that medal? The panic is infectious. Before you know it, somebody is turning to you in the playground and bleating: 'I'm sure that girl's had the medal twice, you know. We've not had it once and my child's on the same reading book as her.'

So before you poke your nose into another child's reading bag, relax. It's not a race. Don't let your own insecurities handicap your child before he even reaches the first hurdle.

PLAYGROUND DISPUTES AND THE MOTHERING MAFIA

You might think you've seen it all. In these days of reality TV, when every other programme features somebody shouting at somebody else, you may feel reasonably unshockable.

You ain't seen nothing yet. Just wait until the first time you see two parents leaping to the defence of their children in a playground dispute. It'll scare the pants off you.

The sheer ferociousness of the tongue-lashing can be quite something to behold. Parents will scream the most outrageous accusations at each other. They'll use language you only ever see on the back of toilet doors. They'll threaten to bring in the police, to sue the school, to have the perpetrator expelled. And never at any point will it cross their minds that their own child may be a teensy-weensy bit to blame.

For head teachers, the mothering mafia are an absolute nightmare. While schools can discipline a child for dropping litter, they have absolutely no authority over two parents who have completely lost it and are trading insults in the middle of a busy playground.

And, of course, it's not always the mums. Often it's dad who rolls up on his high horse, showing his face in the playground for the first time this year, to have a go at some other parent who's probably blissfully unaware of whatever incident has sent his blood pressure soaring this time.

'I've told my lad that if it happens again, he's to thump him back,' he storms. Well, that's that sorted, then.

Nor should you run away with the idea that this is something that only ever happens with the roughhouse parents of the naughtiest boy in class. It could just as easily be that middle-manager, used to throwing his weight around at work, whose sense of apparent injustice leads him to make a total spectacle of himself in front of 200 fascinated children and a whole army of open-mouthed mums.

So, what do you do? Your child comes home with a bruise the size of an apple on his arm and some story about how he was attacked. Just how do you approach the offender's mother the next morning and bring it up in conversation? The answer is, you don't.

The first thing you do is to try to get at the truth and your first question to your child should always be: 'What did you do?' You're going to have egg on your face if you get to school tomorrow, all guns blazing, and the other child has a classic shiner that your child inflicted first.

If you're still convinced that something has happened sufficiently serious to warrant your intervention, go and talk to a member of staff. They will use their generally far superior judgment and experience to get to the bottom of the problem. They are, after all, in a better position to sort it out than two mothers, both with all the instincts that make them want to defend their own child.

Teachers are used to that early-morning head round the door and those well-used words: 'I hope you don't think I'm being a fussy parent, but ...'

Even if the teacher thinks you are a fusspot, they'd rather be kept in the picture than get into a situation where you're greeting your child at the school gates with: 'Are you all right? Did he get you today?' in a way that makes him ever more fearful. Neither do they want you falling out with another parent.

Yes, children can be cruel, they can say and do awful things, and then they can have a cry and say sorry and that will be the end of it. Adults, somewhere along the line, have lost that ability to apologise. When they lose their temper with each other, months can pass before they exchange a civil word again. And what an example to set to their children, who were probably bosom buddies again by the end of the week.

The key things to remember are:

- All children fall out sometimes and the fall-outs can be spectacular.
- All children come home with bruises sometimes. Seeing the mayhem that goes on in playgrounds everywhere, it's amazing they don't come home with far worse.
- Even if something has happened so serious that it warrants further action, losing your temper with another adult won't help.
- By the time you get involved, there's every chance the two children will have kissed and made up.

So when your child comes home tear-stained and with some one-off, unexpected tale of woe, take a step back before you jump in at the deep end. Don't let a children's dispute turn into a parents' quarrel.

FIVE THINGS THAT DRIVE DINNER LADIES CRAZY

1. Parents who send their children to school in winter dressed for the Bahamas in summer. These are the parents who, despite all the yellow zigzags and warning signs, drive so far up the school drive that, if only the classroom doors were open, they'd zoom in, deposit the child, do a handbrake turn, and leave. Their children arrive in school wearing wafer-thin coats, or no coat at all, and then have to spend a freezing lunch hour risking hypothermia while their dad no doubt continues to cruise the town in his climate-controlled car before returning at the end of the school day and pulling into a space marked 'Strictly teaching staff only'. If you drive your child to school, don't forget that he's going to be playing outdoors for a lot of the day, no matter how cold it gets. Children need a warm coat – check the thickness of those sleeves! And, however much she begs and pleads, keep your daughter's strappy sandals and high-heeled boots for weekends. They've no place in a playground.

2. Telltales. How dinner ladies, sorry, midday supervisors, have their patience severely tested by children who are forever shopping each other. 'Miss, Ruth Graves just pushed Sandra Jones. And she did it yesterday as well.' The dinner lady looks over and there are Ruth and Sandra playing quite happily together. Try to teach your child that there's a time to intervene and a time to mind your own business. Nobody loves a telltale.

3. Parents who persist in sending their child to school with a packed

lunch they hate. Some schools adopt the sensible policy of making a child put back into his lunchbox anything he fails to eat. Do parents take the hint? They do not. Despite the fact that their child hates sandwiches, they persist in putting them into the box in the morning and throwing them out at night. If he really won't eat sandwiches, you might just have to find something else.

4. Toys, money and jewellery. The child who comes to school with his pockets stuffed with treasured possessions is destined to lose something before the day is out or at the very least fall out with someone who wants to borrow them. Keep toys for home.

5. Windy days. Who knows what it is about windy weather, but there's something about it that turns children slightly crazy. They charge around like creatures possessed in the playground – and then take a touch of the madness indoors to the obvious delight of the teacher about to embark on his literacy hour.

Those are the gripes, but dinner ladies also have a few words of reassurance for parents fearful of how their child will cope in a seething playground.

Most children, they say, thoroughly enjoy it and few are permanently without a friend.

And while, in this age of plenty for the nation's children, few of us would dream of putting six children into our back gardens and leaving them to play for an hour with perhaps a few hoops and a ball between them, in a playground it seems to work remarkably well.

Devoid of expensive toys and the arguments that go with them, most children fall back on their imagination and dream up their own entertainment. Some sing, some create and perform their own plays, some play traditional playground games just as we once did, and some – the boys, generally – run around pretending to be Sonic or whatever the latest craze happens to be.

Some even discover hidden talents for sporting genius. One five-year-old, who had spent all lunchtime in goal while another boy fired penalties at him, came home full of admiration for his friend's prowess.

'He scored *fifteen* goals!' the child told his mum.

'But I thought you weren't allowed a football?' she said.

'We're not,' said the child. 'It was a pretend ball, but he told me it went in every time.'

9 THE NATIONAL CURRICULUM: KEY STAGE 1

Key Stage 1, the first key stage in the national curriculum in England, is for children aged from five to seven. The aim is that by the end of that first stage, your child should have reached a certain level of knowledge and understanding.

At the end of the stage, seven year olds are given tests in English and maths to check how they're doing. The government uses the results to see how many children are making the hoped-for progress.

So, what do they learn?

ENGLISH

Even for children so young, learning English is far more than working their way through a set of numbered reading books. Yes, they will spend a lot of time learning to read, but they'll also be writing, talking, listening and stretching their imaginations.

Almost all schools have a daily literacy hour when they concentrate on all aspects of English.

The key areas taught are:

- **Speaking and listening:** Just look at the emphasis placed on this – a skill most of us wouldn't even think of as a classroom subject. Children are taught to think about what they say, express themselves clearly, listen to others rather than talk over the top of them, talk with their teacher and classmates and pool their ideas. They'll act, tell stories, read aloud, and describe things that have happened to them.
- **Reading:** The emphasis isn't on how fast you can race through a reading scheme, but on how well you understand what you're reading. Children focus on words and sentences and look at how they fit into the writing. They are asked to work out the meaning of what they're reading and express an opinion about it. And their

reading isn't restricted to storybooks. They also look at plays and poems; learn to digest information given, for example, on computer screens; and use dictionaries and encyclopedias.

Writing: Every aspect of writing is covered to give children a grasp of just how widely used and important it is in everyday life. As well as writing stories and poems, they'll write notes, lists, captions, records, messages and instructions. They'll learn about punctuation, work on turning that enormous writing they did in reception into a clear, neat, legible script, and they'll be taught the patterns of letters and sounds, which will help them spell.

TARGETS

In the three areas mentioned above, by the end of Year Two, most children are expected to be able to:

- **Speaking and listening:** Listen carefully. Speak clearly. Tell stories and repeat poems. Learn new words and use them in conversation. Show they have thought about the people listening to them by adding details to keep them interested. Change how they talk to different people according to the situation.
- **Reading:** Read aloud and be able to understand what they're reading. Express an opinion about what they've read. Use more than one way to work out the meaning of a word they don't know.
- **Writing:** Write stories with a beginning, a middle and an end. Use writing for different reasons, such as giving instructions. Use interesting and relevant vocabulary. Choose words and add in details that will interest the reader. Write in sentences with capital letters at the beginning and full stops at the end. Spell common words correctly. Use spelling patterns to work out how to spell unfamiliar words. Shape letters correctly, and write neatly and clearly.

MATHS

Why do we learn maths? Because we use maths every day, whether we're counting out the dinner money or trying to cut 22 slices from one small Barbie birthday cake.

Almost all schools have a daily maths lesson and children learn about:

- **Number:** Counting, calculating, solving simple problems and making simple lists, tables and charts.

- **Shape, space and measure:** Looking at, exploring and describing the features of shapes like triangles, rectangles, squares, cubes, hexagons, pentagons, cylinders and spheres. Describing positions, directions and movements and right angles. Working and measuring with units of time, length, weight and capacity.

Now you know why maths lessons are no longer the boring, silent lessons we remember from school. Today's children use and apply their maths. They do practical tasks and talk about mathematical problems, reasoning together to find a solution. They learn that maths isn't always about coming up with an exact answer. Estimating a rough answer is an important mathematical skill that helps with problem solving and answer checking.

They do lots of sums in their heads, not least by imagining numbers and the relationships between them, to get them into the habit of doing mental arithmetic before they get into that other mathematical habit – relying on calculators.

TARGETS

Again, by the end of Year Two, most children should be able to:

- **Using and applying maths:** Tackle a problem by choosing a sensible approach. Spot patterns and describe them. Use words, symbols and basic diagrams to record what they do in a mathematical way. Explain what they did to solve a problem.
- **Number:** Count, read and write whole numbers up to 100, and put them in order. Count forwards or backwards in ones or tens from different starting numbers. Tell if numbers are odd or even. Understand that an addition can be undone with a subtraction. Know by heart all the adding and subtracting facts for each number up to ten (in other words, know, for example, that 6 plus 4 equals 10, and that 4 plus 6 still equals 10, etc.). Know the pairs of numbers in tens that make 100 (for instance, 30 plus 70). Know that addition can be tackled in any order and that it's easier to put the biggest number first. Understand that multiplication means the same as adding more of the same number. Double numbers or halve them. Know the two times and ten times tables by heart.
- **Shape, space and measure:** Use the mathematical names for familiar two-dimensional and three-dimensional shapes. Say how many sides and corners there are in a shape and whether there are any right angles. Predict what a shape would look like in a mirror.

Understand turning movements such as whole turns, quarter turns, or right angles. Measure or weigh things using units like centimetres, metres, litres or kilograms, and choose sensible units to use. Use a ruler to draw and measure lines in centimetres. And tell the time to the half- and quarter-hour.

And there's more ...

SCIENCE

All children are curious about the world around them. From the moment they utter their first 'But why?' life can seem one long round of questions. Early science is designed to make the most of that curiosity and give children some answers to all those whys.

Children explore:

- **Life processes and living things:** Like familiar animals and plants
- **Materials and their properties:** Things like wood, paper and rock
- **Physical processes:** The basics of physics, taught through their discoveries with electricity, forces, light and sounds

The emphasis is on scientific enquiry. The teacher (or sometimes the children) asks questions, and then the children work together to find the answer by discovering facts and recording their work. Then they look at whether what they did was a sensible way of going about finding the answer. They also use reference books and computer sources, and then they use scientific language, drawings, charts and tables to record their work, sometimes on computers.

TARGETS

By the end of Year Two most children should be able to:

- **Scientific enquiry:** Suggest how they can find out about a scientific question. Look for the information they need, whether from a book or their own observations. Think about what they have discovered and compare it with what they expected. Look at and compare objects and living things, then classify them according to a description such as 'hard' or 'soft'.
- **Life processes and living things:** Describe what a plant or animal needs to survive. Understand that all living things eat, grow and reproduce. Grasp that different plants and animals live in different habitats.

- **Materials and their properties:** Sort materials into groups according to their properties, such as 'rough' or 'smooth'. Describe how some materials change when, for instance, they are heated.
- **Physical processes:** Illuminate a bulb using a simple circuit with a battery and switch. Compare the brightness and colour of lights, and the loudness or pitch of sounds. Describe moving objects by talking about their speed and direction.

DESIGN AND TECHNOLOGY

Another dream subject for the 'but why?' brigade. Design and technology gives children the chance to explore how familiar products and objects actually work and teaches them how to solve practical problems.

Children are taught to:

- Look at and talk about familiar products (made of materials such as card, textiles and food) to see how they work
- Use simple skills such as cutting and gluing to make their own products
- Use their new knowledge to plan and make their own things

TARGETS

By the end of Year Two most children should be able to:

- Develop ideas for design and technology products, talk about their ideas and plan the next step, and choose and use the equipment and methods they need
- Put together materials and components in different ways
- Talk about how they could improve their future work

INFORMATION AND COMMUNICATION TECHNOLOGY

This covers computers and more. Children are taught everything from how to use the Internet to how to take granny's picture with a digital camera.

Children learn how to use ICT to gather, share and exchange information. They become familiar with some hardware and software. They keep information on computers, learn to present it in different ways, and talk about how ICT can be used in the classroom and beyond.

TARGETS

By the end of Year Two most children should be able to: use ICT to handle information in different ways; start to get used to using computers in their everyday schoolwork; use computerised instructions to help them construct a programmable toy; and explore what happens using ICT.

HISTORY

Children learn about the lives of people from British and world history. As well as looking at important events, they also look at their own history – how they have changed in their seven years and how their parents' lives have changed.

TARGETS

By the end of Year Two most children should: Use words about time passing, such as 'a long time ago'. Realise that some things happened before anyone living now was born. Start to understand why people acted as they did. Realise that their own lives are different to those of children from the past. See that the past has been represented in different ways.

GEOGRAPHY

Children start to use maps and plans to find out about places, not least the area around their school.

TARGETS

By the end of Year Two most children should be able to: Describe the main features of places they study. Understand that some places are similar and others different from each other. Recognise where things are and why. Spot changes in an area they study. Grasp the impact of people on the environment. Find out about and give their views on places.

OTHER SUBJECTS TAUGHT INCLUDE:

Art and design: Children are taught to explore and develop their ideas. They try out different materials, tools and techniques. They talk about their work and that of their peers.

Music: Children learn how to sing and play musical instruments. They explore sounds and create their own music. They learn to listen and describe how sounds change.

Physical Education: Children learn dance, which teaches them to move rhythmically and expressively and use their imaginations. They play games, using their skills to score points or goals. They practise gymnastics.

Religious Education: Children are taught about the main religions in this country, particularly Christianity. The aim is to help children respect the beliefs of others as well as finding out more about their own. All schools must teach religious education, but there is no national study that all must follow. Most follow a local education authority programme though some, such as church schools, may follow a different programme. You are entitled to remove your child from all or part of religious education if you feel that is in his best interests.

Personal, Social and Health Education and Citizenship: Not a compulsory subject, though the government encourages schools to include it. Sometimes taught as part of other subjects, it aims to teach children to take responsibility for their own health and wellbeing, and to respect and get on with others.

If your child is tired and his teacher stressed, that's probably given you a fair idea of why. To think that some of these children will still be six when they're expected to know all that.

10 HOW TIMES CHANGE

Cast your mind back to your own schooldays. Unless you're one of those mothers who demoralise the rest of us by turning up at the school gates looking young enough to be our daughters, the chances are you'll recognise something from this.

THE BAD OLD DAYS

Hands up – sitting up straight at the back there, please – anyone who can remember primary school teachers who ruled by humiliation. Oh, yes, who could ever forget the dreaded weekly maths test that decided your fate for the week to come. Remember how the teacher would announce your results from the top position down, allocating your seat for the following week according to how well you'd scored, how quickly you could bring to mind that seven eights were – well, whatever seven eights were. And when was the last time you needed to know?

Not only was this immensely nerve-racking, it was also unbearably harsh. We all grew to dislike the smug devils who never once left the top table. And we could never meet the eye of the poor lad with all the numerical ability of the Flower Pot Men who remained resolutely glued to the dunce's chair on the table of shame.

And if that rings no bells, what about this? Remember queuing up at the teacher's desk waiting, endlessly waiting, for her to look over your work or hear you read? Can you picture it now, that snake of bored children waiting for that precious moment of one-to-one attention while the rest of the class did what? Messed about, more often than not, with their games interspersed by brief flurries of writing when the teacher looked up and lashed them with a tongue of pure venom.

Classrooms then were silent places where lessons were all chalk and little but the teacher's talk. Children were expected to learn by rote and speak only if spoken to.

Their work was a mystery to their parents and certainly a mystery to their classmates. They were encouraged to develop a bizarre knack for writing while one arm shielded their notes from prying eyes and their nose hovered three inches from the desk for fear that their nearest neighbour might catch a glimpse of what they'd learned. It was all about as much fun as sago pudding.

Goodbye to the bad old days, hello modern learning.

TEACHING TODAY

Today's classrooms are a million miles from the schools of the past. The most obvious change is that there's a buzz of busy noise.

Children are no longer encouraged to work alone in an impenetrable bubble of confusion. Increasingly, children work in groups, pooling their knowledge to learn from each other. They're learning in an almost adult way, bouncing ideas off each other and problem-solving together much as their parents might back at the office.

They're taught from the earliest age to develop the skills that will make them independent learners. Children are instructed not to sit around with their arm in the air waiting for the teacher's attention. It's drummed into them that time is precious and if they're stuck they should have another go at solving the problem, or ask a classmate for help, or do something else productive until the teacher is free.

To parents brought up in an era when education was, broadly speaking, something to be tolerated rather than enjoyed, the changes take some getting used to. Most of us can see the benefits – with one exception.

'Whatever happened to one-to-one reading?' we moan. 'The teacher hardly ever listens to him read on his own. In my day ...'

Well, it's not our day any more. Children generally now read in groups, and it's no longer just about rattling through three pages before playtime. They might read a paragraph each. They might pause to work out together what a new word could mean. Then, as a group, they could discuss the story – why the witch got her comeuppance, why it made everyone laugh, and why there's a question mark at the bottom of page three.

The emphasis now is not just on reading, but more on children understanding what they've read.

And if you still think your child is missing out on one-to-one reading, there's an easy answer to that. Let him read to you!

INFORMATION TECHNOLOGY

If you're one of those parents who think computers are for others, read on.

Nothing has changed education quite like information and communication technology. The advent of ICT has meant not so much an evolution as a revolution in the way children learn.

With the whole world now literally at their fingertips, computers have helped to bring learning alive. And if that's what it's done for the generation now leaving university, imagine what it has to offer our children only now taking their first steps on the learning journey.

It's all immensely confusing for those of us brought up by a generation which firmly believed that calculators were a great evil, destined to stop children thinking, and putting an end to the dubious delights of long division. But unless we make the effort to understand at least the basics of computer skills, a huge and important chunk of our children's education will remain a mystery to us. And this is why:

- Computers are infiltrating every aspect of our children's learning. If you thought computers were something they did for an hour every Friday afternoon, think again. They're being used in virtually every subject in ways you wouldn't believe.
- Even the youngest children will start to learn computer skills. And before you know it, they'll be using those skills to improve their spelling, composition, maths, art work, and the rest. And, while in some schools computers are still not being used as often as they could be, the general push is to get children using them more and more.
- The pace of change is frightening. Even the IT specialists in primary schools are hard-pressed to keep up with the constant bombardment of new advances. As soon as they invest in one piece of kit, there's another – faster, more powerful, more impressive – coming off the production line. If they bought everything they'd like, the school would be bankrupt and the PTA on its knees.
- Computers are going to play an enormous role in the whole lives of our children. They are not going to be something they use at school and never need again. This isn't O level German. This is learning for life. Whether our children grow up to be prime ministers or lawyers or plumbers or cooks, they will still need computers. Unless you believe your mum was right when she pooh-poohed the purchase of your first calculator, you really owe it to your child at least to learn the basics.

HOW DO PRIMARY SCHOOLS USE COMPUTERS?

Every which way. Many schools now have a bank of computers, their own IT suite, where a whole class can use the resource together. Sometimes they'll work on one piece of work simultaneously, and in other lessons they'll work individually or in pairs on a program that might, for instance, test their spelling.

Each computer gives them access to a vast and endless library. Through the Internet they can find information on any topic under the sun, just like that. It is normal practice for schools to have filtered Internet systems so that children cannot gain access to unsuitable material. Many schools go so far as to seek written permission from parents for their children to have Internet access. If you have any concerns, ask about the Internet policy at your child's school.

They can also reach out to the rest of the world. Remember those interminable geography lessons we had to endure in which we learned about the lives of people in Africa we could neither see nor, frankly, did we care about?

Well, imagine what it's like for today's pupils. They can learn about another country and another culture from the horse's mouth. They can talk to children in an African school through the Internet. They can use e-mails to build up links, exchange pictures, talk about each other's lives, swap ideas. Suddenly, the rest of the world isn't remote at all. It's immediate and vibrant and interesting.

And just because children are using computers, working on educational programs flashing up before them on a computer screen, it doesn't mean they have to be heads down, working in a world of their own while the teacher paces around behind them with nothing to do but answer requests for the toilet. (Ah, if only, says the teacher.) Computers are fabulous tools for group learning.

Many primary schools have invested in white boards, which basically look like an enormous computer screen. Imagine, for instance, that the class is using a white board for a maths lesson. Up might come a picture of a supermarket shelf with the prices of fruit marked underneath. The task is to buy an apple, four pears and a banana. So up comes little Johnny from his seat and he works out that he owes 83p. He touches the pound coin at the bottom of the screen and he drags it by touching it with his finger up to the till. Then he dips in the till and drags out, coin by coin, his 17p change. All done by pictures, all on a screen, and not a computer mouse in sight.

It's clever stuff. And in the time it's taken to write this, somebody's probably invented something even better.

There are no limits to the scope for using computers in education. History projects spring to life with moving images and fingertip facts. There's design, science, art, music, and on and on it goes.

Even from the youngest age, children are using technology. Through play tills, metal detectors, floor robots, they're learning how to make technology work for them.

By the age of seven, most children can use ICT to handle information in different ways. They learn to find information, store it, sort it, and present it to others. It's already become routine for them to use computer software in their everyday work, perhaps writing and changing their class work and jazzing it up with some fancy design. And if that's what they can do at seven, just imagine what they'll be doing at seventeen.

BUT I HATE COMPUTERS!

Are you sure, or is it just that 'mum and the calculator' syndrome rearing its ugly head again?

Lots of parents claim to hate computers, but what they really mean is that they hate the idea of learning about them. If the only computer you saw as a child was in Dr Who's Tardis, take heart. There are thousands of us out there.

Too many of those of us old enough to remember the Daleks belong to a generation trapped in a time warp. Our children know about computers, the younger parents at our children's school know all about computers, embarrassingly our own parents have often used their newfound free time to learn about them, yet some of us still feel like the dinosaurs in the sandwich, struggling to master the video controls.

If you're serious about helping your child through the learning maze, it makes sense to drag yourself into the 21st century and get some basic computer skills. It needn't be a huge commitment. There are lots of free computer courses out there, offering short courses to get you started. You'll be amazed by what this might open up for you. You might even catch up with your child and be able to explore the mind-blowing world of computers together.

While the price of basic entry-level computers has never been lower (and is still falling), if your biggest worry is still that you don't have and can't afford a computer, don't let that put you off. The government has invested colossal sums in ensuring that there is computer access for all. Libraries now offer access to computers and the Internet, often free. They are also often good sources of information for anyone wanting to take free computer courses.

Go on, pluck up the courage and give it a whirl. Don't be that parent who says what teachers hear all too often. 'We've got a computer, but I don't even know how to switch it on,' mum boasts. 'I know how to dust it though! Anyway, if I did have a go, I just know I'd delete everything!' Bet her mum hated calculators, too.

> I thought I was computer literate, I thought I was all right, until I saw my daughter going click, click, click on the computer and sorting something out while I was still trying to understand the instructions. It made me realise how much I need to take a computer course.
>
> *The mother of a six-year-old*

11 FORMAL TESTS

National testing of children starts remarkably early. Children in England face their first national curriculum tests, commonly known as SATs, when they are six or seven. They have a second round just before they leave primary school.

And, if the very thought sends a chill down your spine, rest assured that you are not alone. Many teachers loathe them, too.

Yet even schools that would gladly see them abolished tomorrow have no choice but to take them seriously. How children fare in the SATs they take in Year Six determines the school's ratings in the infamous league tables. Like it or not, they're stuck with them.

How teachers prepare children varies enormously from school to school. Some pile on the extra work. They encourage parents to help their children revise and are happy to see them using all those 'Help your child to succeed in SATs' books that test the nerves of even the coolest parents.

Other schools do the opposite. They take the view that children, particularly of six and seven, should not be put under so much pressure, that a full day at school followed by homework is more than enough, particularly for a child who is still in the infants.

But where does that leave parents? Caught in a soup of indecision, they don't know whether they should be playing the tests down or building them up. Well, here are the facts, so judge for yourself.

KEY STAGE 1 TESTS

The first SATs your child will face come at the end of Key Stage 1, which covers the learning years for children aged five to seven.

WHY TEST CHILDREN SO YOUNG?

The aim is to measure what all children can do when they are set the same questions.

Then, so the theory goes, the school can do its best by your child because the results give it valuable information on how well he is doing. They show both you and the teachers your child's strengths and weaknesses and help you plan ahead.

Critics would argue that a good teacher is well aware of how a child is doing without the need for such regimented testing and that they would be planning ahead anyway.

WHAT ARE THE TESTS LIKE?

The way seven-year-olds in England are assessed changed in 2004. Out went the inflexibility of a rigid testing system and in came a new way of assessing how children had progressed.

Under the old system, seven-year-olds were both tested and assessed separately by their teachers and parents were given two sets of results – one showing how their children had performed in their tests, the other showing what level of work they were achieving in the classroom day to day.

The new system retains the tests, but brings in more flexibility for when and how they are administered. The test results form part of the whole assessment of a child's progress. Parents receive just one overall result.

The changes were made because the government recognised what many teachers had been saying all along – that a teacher's overall, rounded assessment of a child's progress throughout the year, backed up by national testing, gives a much more accurate picture of how a child is really doing than relying on their performance in one set of tests alone.

Forget the terminology – task or test, it makes little difference. All are ways of assessing your child's progress. A task might, for instance, involve your child reading to an adult who will assess his reading skills. For most children, the English tests will cover reading, writing and spelling. As in any formal exam, the children sit apart from each other and are not allowed help.

The same applies in maths. Children are given a booklet and work their way through it. The test might include questions on addition, subtraction, multiplication, division, graphs, money, shapes and problem solving. And, yes, many of the children will still be just *six*.

Less able children will do tasks more appropriate to their level of skill. Some will be judged on teacher assessment alone.

WHAT HAPPENS IF THEY FAIL?

Panic not. This is not a pass or fail test. What the tests assess is the level of achievement your child has reached at the end of the first stage of the national curriculum.

A child who has reached Level 1 at age seven will be judged to have performed below expectations. Levels 2a, 2b and 2c are the expected levels of achievement. Level 3 is beyond expectations, and Level 4 exceptional.

Children who are not achieving above Level 2c at this stage may not reach level 4 – the expected achievement – by the age of eleven.

HOW CAN I HELP MY CHILD DO WELL?

Exactly the same way you've been helping him since he was born. Be encouraging, be loving, be supportive. Praise him when he does well with any of his schoolwork and take an interest in what's happening. Move heaven and earth to make sure you attend whatever meeting the school might arrange to inform parents about the tests.

And try to ensure he's not going to school tired. Children who turn up to school already tired can't possibly do their best.

You can, of course, do all those other popular learning tricks – getting your child to tot up the numbers on car registration plates when you're stuck in traffic, asking how much change he'll need when he pays for a bag of sweets, talking to him about the way things work.

And read, read, read. A child of nine or more will ideally read quietly for twenty minutes a day. An adult should, in a perfect world, read with a younger child for around the same time.

But these are habits that should be routine, not something you do intensively for a fortnight before a test.

HOW MUCH PRESSURE SHOULD I EXPECT FROM THE SCHOOL, AND SHOULD I FOLLOW THEIR LEAD?

There's a very good case for saying that children of six and seven should be put under no additional pressure at all. Resist the lure of all those Key Stage 1 revision books. Your child will be under quite enough pressure at school without you giving him three hours a night mental arithmetic on top.

Avoid using the word 'tests'. Call them 'special work' if you have to refer to them at all. And stress to your child that the only important thing to you is that he does his best. No one can ask more than that.

KEY STAGE 2 TESTS

The tests for ten- and eleven-year-olds usually take place in early May. Children are tested in English, maths and science – and pretty thoroughly tested, too.

These are the first national tests that really hit them between the eyes. Most seven-year-olds are blissfully unaware of all the hype surrounding SATs, but by the time they get to Year Six there's no disguising the fact that this is serious stuff.

Over the years in between, most schools choose to set their children optional end-of-year tests to check on their progress. They help children get used to being tested formally, but nothing can prepare them for the shock of the real thing.

With those final primary tests looming, this is when – for some children – the sleepless nights begin, the tears and tantrums emerge as nerves are frayed by pressure piling in from all sides.

Head teachers and class teachers alike are under tremendous pressure to ensure children do well in these tests. The school's reputation and its standing in the league tables depends on how the children perform.

It's at this stage that some schools allow more of that pressure than is reasonable to filter down to the pupils. Some start months before, setting children past papers, gearing them up for the tests as though the children's whole futures depended on them.

However much pressure your child appears to be under at school, do try as a parent to keep the whole business of SATs in perspective. Support him, of course, help him through what may be one of the most testing times of his school life so far, encourage him to do his best, but do remember that his whole future does not rest on the results.

Ironically, looking at the tests purely from the child's point of view, in some cases the results have relatively little immediate impact. While some secondary schools use the results to stream children, others say they come too late to help with their forward planning for the new intake. By the time the results are out, some secondary schools have done all their initial grading and setting and their students have generally been allocated their classes. For them, it's too late for the SATs to count.

You could argue that, for all the pressure that comes with the SATs, a child who has sweated and toiled to get a high score is mainly rewarded by knowing that his parting shot helped his old school. His efforts will have influenced the school's position in those all-important tables. And somewhere down the line, the parents of a four-year-old may be using those same results to determine their own child's future schooling.

WHAT TEN- AND ELEVEN-YEAR-OLDS SHOULD ACHIEVE

By their final year in primary school, children who have achieved Level 4 have reached the level expected for their age. Level 5 would mean they had performed beyond expectations.

Looking ahead for a moment, they will face further tests at fourteen, when children are expected to have reached Level 5 or 6. Level 7 would be beyond expectations, and 8 – the top grade – exceptional.

WHY TEACHERS HATE SATS

A sweeping generalisation, maybe, but few tears would be shed in educational circles if the tests were scrapped.

There are several reasons why the tests are unpopular with teachers:

1. They put them under tremendous pressure. For the Year Six teacher, there's the constant stress of knowing that her school's standing in the tables rests on her ability to get her class to perform well in the tests and meet their targets. And those targets keep on getting tougher. In larger primaries, where there might be several classes in the same year, she has the additional strain of trying to match the performance of her colleagues.
2. Teachers, quite rightly, feel uneasy about passing that pressure down to young children. They have somehow to drum into the children and their parents that the results matter without hyping the whole thing totally out of proportion. It's not easy for them to get across the 'don't worry' message when it's patently obvious that they're pretty worried about it themselves.
3. Teachers argue that, in the most test-obsessed schools, the staff are encouraged to 'teach to the tests'. Children spend, they say, a disproportionate amount of their time being taught how to pass the tests at the expense of other things.
4. The tables give a skewed view of schools. Teachers argue that parents who look at the results in isolation, without taking into account, for instance, the area a school serves, cannot get a true picture of the standard of teaching.

And the tests, like all tests, don't always do justice to an individual child. A child may have performed badly for any one of a number of reasons, from illness to sheer terror.

Taken together, both test results and assessments, you should have a clearer idea of how your child has progressed.

AND FINALLY...

As a parent, the most important thing to bear in mind is that SATs are not GCSEs. For you and your child, they're simply an assessment of where he's at and where his education needs to go from here.

The results should come as no surprise. They should simply confirm what you know of your child, from what you see and what your teacher tells you. If he's exceptionally bright, they should show that. If he's chugging along in the mainstream, at the level most children reach by his age, then that's what his test should show.

SATs are not an exercise in fast-tracking him to Cambridge. As much as anything, they're a check on the school to make sure it is doing its job.

For all we grumble, most of us can't resist looking at those tables when it comes to choosing a school for our child. And you can bet your bottom dollar that most teachers do the same when they're looking around for a new post.

What you have to do, on your child's behalf, is keep the whole thing in proportion. The worst sin you could commit would be to stand in the playground in front of your child and others comparing results with other parents.

If you know your child tried his best, even if the result was disappointing, put it behind you and move on. There's always another key stage waiting for you just around the corner.

My son was aware of the tests, but I was glad that the school didn't overemphasise them and pile on too much pressure.
The mother of a nine-year-old

I think it's outrageous, absolutely outrageous, that these tests are inflicted on what are still little children. I'm sure I will be worried about it when our time comes.
The mother of a six-year-old girl

It's bizarre that we put our children through all this at seven, the age when in Scandinavian countries children are only just starting school.
The parent of a five-year-old boy

---

12 HOMEWORK

If we mean it when we say that we want school and parents to work in partnership, then homework is surely our side of the bargain.

Teachers do what they can to encourage our children to learn, but without our support it's an uphill struggle. That's why homework is so crucial in giving children that extra spurt throughout their formal education.

But be warned. Homework will test your resolve like nothing else. Unless you get it right, it will become a nightly chore or, worse still, a battleground. And that's no good to anyone.

WHY HOMEWORK MATTERS FROM THE START

No teacher, however wonderful, can possibly give as much one-to-one attention as children ideally need. Of course she'll hear your child read. Of course she'll listen to him recite his new word list, but she may well have 29 other children all with an equal right to her time.

And there's your little boy, desperate to read the next exciting instalment of *Roger Red Hat* and show just how clever he is, and it might not even be his turn until tomorrow. This is a child who has only just started school, who is used to being the centre of attention, who loves his books. If he wants a story, he's used to sitting down and showing off to mum there and then.

What he needs when he gets home is a mum and dad who are desperately interested in how he's doing. To the child, it's obviously nowhere near as good as praise from teacher, the new demigod, but it'll do.

Teachers rely on the help you give. At the beginning, when a child's homework may be learning a handful of new letters or words, the work you do with your child at home really does make a difference. Only you have the opportunity to keep getting those words out of the tin and repeating them over and over again. Only you can do it the proper way, in short bursts when you've got your child's attention.

You can do it over breakfast, you can do it at the weekend, you can do it in the car on the way to grandma's. Just ten minutes, here and there, getting your child familiar with those words, kick-starting those reading skills.

And, while the new words they learn will help your child enormously with his reading, he's also learning just as much from the fact that you bother at all. The message you're giving is that you're interested, that you think he's doing really well, that this is something worth your time and his. And that's more valuable than a thousand Roger Red Hats (Sorry, Rog).

HOW *NOT* TO DO HOMEWORK

It is so easy to get a young child's homework wrong. Parents spend so much time worrying that they'll teach their child to read 'the wrong way', when really that's the least of their worries. What matters is their attitude to homework, and their attitude to their child.

Treat your child's homework like some major inconvenience in your day and what is the child to make of it? It won't take him long to get the message that homework doesn't matter to you and shouldn't matter to him.

So, a few don'ts:

- **Don't do homework with the television on:** He won't concentrate and neither will you.
- **Don't sit him down to do it before he's even unzipped his coat:** The poor child's been at school all day. He wants a drink and a chance to unwind. He doesn't want to learn twenty words before he's allowed within stacking distance of his Lego.
- **Don't pretend it doesn't matter:** 'He's only four, for goodness' sake. He comes home and he's tired. There'll be time enough for homework next year.' We sympathise, but it's *now* when he's trying to learn to read and it's now he needs the help. It's a bit like learning to ride a bike. If you only get on it once a week, it's going to take a long time. A little bit of practice every day goes a long way.
- **Don't put all the responsibility on the teacher:** 'She's the expert. I don't know what I'm doing. Besides, it's her job. I don't see why I should do it for her.' Well, yes, it is her job, but it's your child and your job, too.

- **Don't get cross:** This may be the fourth night in a row that he's got stuck on the word 'goat', but this is difficult stuff. Keep your cool. As long as he's trying, that's good enough.
- **Don't let homework become a battleground:** It's so easy to fall into the trap of spending more time arguing over when you're going to do homework than actually doing it.
- **Don't become a slave to homework:** Of course it's important, but it isn't something you have to do absolutely every night. If the child is going to a birthday party that finishes at seven, don't force an exhausted child to do homework at bedtime. It won't hurt to skip homework sometimes. And on the days when your child is really beside himself with tiredness, there's absolutely no rule that says it can't be done in the morning.

HOW TO DO HOMEWORK WELL

The first and good news is that homework for small children should be mercifully brief. Little and often is the rule. You can't expect a five-year-old to concentrate for a long time at the end of a full school day. Ask your teacher for advice – most schools should have a written homework policy anyway – but as a general rule ten minutes should be about right.

Give them a chance to unwind but let them know that homework isn't forgotten. 'We'll have a drink, shall we, and see if we can finish that Lego model? Then we'll do homework and then we'll have tea.' Try to establish the ground rules and it should minimise the opportunities for kicking up a fuss later.

Then, when homework time comes, make sure they've got your full attention. Homework isn't something you should be doing while iron-ing with one hand and cooking pasta with another. Try to give younger siblings something to keep them occupied. They should come to understand that this is special time for you and the older child.

And it should be special. Much as children love to moan about home-work, most secretly quite enjoy the sense of importance, the grown-up feeling it gives them. Showing off to mum is, after all, something all children are programmed to do.

Showing off to dad can be even more special, particularly if mum is the usual wielder of the homework stick. Even if dad isn't around early in the evenings, even if dad doesn't live at home, try to make time for him to be the person who does homework with the child sometimes. Encouragement from one parent is good, from two is twice as nice.

And praise from a teacher is priceless. If you feel your child has worked particularly hard, let the teacher know. Many schools have a homework book that goes backwards and forwards between parent and teacher each day. As well as giving instructions on what homework to do, the teacher may well write in comments about how your child is progressing. It's a good idea to add your own comments. If you feel your child has made a real leap forward in one area, write it down.

It needn't be something earth-shattering. If your child is finding homework hard but is really trying, that itself is worth recording.

The teacher looks in the book, tells the child what mum has written, praises the child, gives him a sticker, he comes home like the cat who got the cream and you're delighted. Your child's confidence and self-esteem are sky high and he wants to do well again. And so it goes on. Unless ...

HOMEWORK AND THE RELUCTANT LEARNER

Sometimes it seems that no matter what you do, homework just becomes one long battle. Children are not stupid. They know that they've got you over a barrel with this one. If your child is a reluctant learner, you'll recognise the scenario.

He digs his heels in and says he's not going to do his homework. You dig your heels in and say he has no choice, and before you know it both sides are so entrenched that the whole situation is impossible. You can't, after all, teach a child to differentiate his boats from his goats if his eyes are raised skywards in a paddy of indifference the minute the homework appears.

This is the time to call in the demigod. Go alone and talk to his teacher. Explain what's happening and ask for advice.

A word from her could be enough to turn the whole thing around. The chances are she'll talk to him about how worried you are. She'll explain why homework is so important and she'll tell him that she'll be talking to you again the next week to see if things have improved. A teacher worth her salt might even offer some kind of reward – yes, possibly even one of those priceless smiley face stickers – by way of incentive.

If he does knuckle down, make sure you give him the praise he's earned. Even if he doesn't seem to be making much headway, the fact that he's trying is the key thing. Never criticise a child for doing their best.

And always make sure that if he is making a real effort, the teacher knows it. A word or two of encouragement from her might be all it takes to break the cycle. Make no mistake, that sulky child in the corner who claims he never wants to read, *ever,* wants your approval just as much as the high-fliers. Get him on a winning streak and he won't want to get off.

HOMEWORK FOR OLDER CHILDREN

Every parent dreads that scary day when their child arrives with homework that is beyond them. Beyond the parent, that is, not the child.

Unless you're a particularly bright spark yourself, expect that moment to come sooner rather than later. Sadly, this is not your excuse to give up and leave them to it. An eight-year-old could easily have thirteen years of study ahead of him. If you plead ignorance now and abandon him to his fate, he's got an awful lot of solitary toil to face.

Many mums, surprisingly, are particularly guilty of copping out once their children reach the juniors. The same mothers who were happy to spend hours teaching letters and numbers to a three-year-old lose their confidence when the going gets tough.

'Ask your Dad,' they tell their nine-year-olds. And later, in comes dad, who has not the foggiest idea what the child is talking about either, but tries bluffing to save face. Suddenly, that home–school partnership is looking rocky in the extreme.

It needn't. Remember, there is absolutely no reason why you should remember the finer points of long division if you haven't practised them in thirty years. You are not alone in no longer having even the vaguest idea what a preposition is.

What is important is that you don't give up. Don't try bluffing. Come clean with your child. Explain that it's a long time since you were at school, that your knowledge of the Romans is a little shaky. Say that, even so, you'd love to learn about them together. Then enlist all the help you can get.

- Ask the child's teacher to show you the modern way of teaching maths. Better still, ask her to do a session with all the interested parents so that you can take heart from your mutual ignorance.

- Go to the library with your child and choose some reference books together.
- Use the Internet. If you don't have a computer at home, use the library's.
- Ask your child. He will delight in showing you all he knows if you'll let him.

Never feel that your child will judge you for your lack of knowledge. He'll just be pleased you're showing an interest. And how pleased with himself is he going to be if he can do long division better than you.

> My children enjoy doing homework. I think they like that time when they know they have my full attention.
>
> *The mother of an infant and a junior*
>
> We don't do homework every night, maybe two or three times a week. Part of the reason I do it is because I want to work in partnership with the teacher. You want to do it for her as well as for your child.
>
> *The mother of six-year-old twins*

13 HELPING YOUR CHILD TO LEARN

So, what is the best way that you can help your child to thrive at school?

READING

In every possible area of education, reading is the key.

So crucial is the skill that a child who can't read can't easily open the doors to science or maths or history or geography. Only when the basic reading blocks are in place can a child begin to access that whole world of information that's out there, waiting to be discovered.

But reading is a truly devilish skill to learn. To all but the most gifted child, learning to read is a slog. Even when they've mastered all those letters and have some vague knowledge of the difference between 'p' and 'q', there are word tins and word lists and shelves groaning with stacks of tedious books to face.

And parents, for sure, forget just how hard the whole process can be. To a child of two, a page of print must be the equivalent of us trying to read a newspaper in Chinese. It's squiggles on a page, nothing more.

Two years later, we expect them to be able to recognise all those squiggles, interpret them into sounds, and build them into words. It's a massive leap. No wonder some children find it hard. The mystery is why more don't.

As parents, it's easy to become obsessed by our children's progress in reading. This is one skill that every parent wants their child to grasp and to grasp with lightning speed. In reality, most of us will need the patience of an exceptionally literate saint to get through the first year of school without screaming at least once: 'It's b, b, b for bus, not d. We just had that in the last word. And the one before – b, b, b.'

If you've ever wondered whether teachers earned their keep, you won't any more.

So, just how do you teach a child to learn to read without at any stage losing your temper, going ga-ga, or giving up? This is how.

BABIES

Learning to read starts with a love of books. And a love of books can start as soon as a baby is old enough to have a fair stab at eating one.

You can't introduce children to books too soon. As soon as a baby is taking notice of the world around them, they're old enough to be given a book. Board and bath books make excellent toys. They can cut their teeth on them, whack their brother with them, they may even look at the pictures in them. Already they're learning how to open books, turn pages, and find something interesting inside.

PRE-SCHOOLERS

Most toddlers love books and stories, not least because time spent reading is usually a quiet, special, snugly time with an adult they love. Many have a voracious appetite for books. Given half a chance, they'll listen to books for as long as you'll read – and not only to delay bed-time either.

Try to make reading part of your daily routine. It will not only build your child's concentration skills, it's a great way to relax and unwind for both of you.

And it'll start to build your own all-important patience levels for the task ahead. Children often become particularly attached to a favourite book, which they'll want to hear over and over again. But, as Thomas the Tank Engine runs into that snowstorm for the tenth time this week, you can at least console yourself with the knowledge that this is a good sign.

A child who gets to know a story inside out is becoming more familiar with words. He'll join in with the parts he knows and eventually come to recognise some of the words on the page. It also reinforces the message that stories are fun – not necessarily for you in this instance, granted, but you could at least try not to let it show.

If you want to increase his enjoyment fivefold, try getting some of that favourite story wrong. His indignation will know no bounds if you swap James for Percy or turn Thomas green. Try missing out even the smallest word and he'll know. And nothing will give him greater pleasure than to point out your mistake.

For your own sanity, you really should consider joining your local library. Joining is free and borrowing books costs nothing either. Even the youngest children can have their own ticket and you can go home staggering under a pile of new books that, with luck, might just send Thomas into the sidings for an hour or two.

Let your child choose at least some of the books himself. He's much more likely to want to read books he had a hand in choosing. You might even go mad and splash out the small cost of hiring books with story tapes – perfect for long journeys.

Many libraries run story times that give young children a chance to sit and enjoy books together. It all reinforces the message that reading is fun.

TOP TIPS FOR YOUNG CHILDREN: Children are much more eager to learn to read if they see how much the adults around them enjoy reading. Make a big issue of your own love of books. Get some books out of the library for yourself when you take your child to make his selection. Even if you never find the time to get beyond chapter two, he'll never know.

Let your child see you reading the newspaper, point out pictures of interest to them – rocket launches, volcanoes, weather stories, the latest outfit from Britney Spears – then read them the story. They'll feel terribly grown-up.

And let them see how reading matters in everyday life. Children's menus are excellent for showing children words and pictures that mean something to them. Ask the manager nicely, and he might even let you take one home for some excellent role-play.

LEARNING TO READ

Every social circle has one – the parent whose child was a fluent reader *before* they went to school. Well, good for them, some children really are ready to make that leap before school is ready to take them. Most are not, so don't panic. There are no prizes for getting there first.

If you have instilled in your child a love of books, if he's grasped that words on a page read from top to bottom and from left to right, he's already on the starting blocks.

Most children learn to read by making the link between letters and sounds. Once they know the sounds that letters make, they grasp how the letters join together to make words. If your child has already made that link and is starting to read by the time they go to school, it would be a strange welcome indeed if their first teacher wasn't delighted.

If your child can recognise and say the sounds of at least some letters, they're also well on their way. Hearing those sounds is a crucial first step, so get playing those word games:

- **Good old 'I Spy':** How many parents have whiled away ten minutes looking for something beginning with 'j' only to find the answer was 'jrink'? The more you play, the better they'll get. Honest.
- **Rhyming words:** How many words can you think of that rhyme with 'cat'?
- **Odd one out:** In a list of 'sit', 'mit', 'hit' and 'cat', which is the odd one out?
- **Singing:** Oh, no, it's that song tape again. All together now: 'Mary, Mary, quite contrary . . .' Spot those rhyming words!

THE BIG LEAP

Somewhere between the ages of four and seven, most children make that leap between recognising the odd word and reading proper.

They will become more confident with the key words that turn up over and over again. And the more key words they recognise at a glance, the greater the chance of them starting to build sentences.

It's a bit like trying to find the answer to a puzzle from a few clues. At first they might look at a sentence and recognise 'the' and 'on' from their word tin. They might see that the second word starts with 'c' and that there's a picture of a cat above it. So if that says 'cat' and the next word looks similar but starts with 's' that could be the rhyming word 'sat'. 'The cat sat on the – must be mat.' Cracked it.

And so the skill builds. A bit of knowledge, a bit of common sense, a grasp of the basic rules and a touch of guesswork. As adult readers, we use the same skills all the time.

Individual children's reading skills develop in different ways. You may find you have:

- **A perfectionist:** This is the child who wants to get every word right and reads painfully slowly. They might need some encouragement to keep the story moving and worry a bit less about the odd mistake. As their reading skills improve, a good tip for discouraging stilted reading is to move your finger along underneath the text at a reasonable pace. They'll want to keep up with you and it works like magic to improve the fluency of their reading.

- **A speed-reader:** This is the child who blasts through a story at 100 mph, occasionally hitting on an accurate word as they go. Not to be overly discouraged at the beginning, but you may then need to try to slow them down and get them to look more carefully at each word.

. . . but chances are you'll have something in between.

Don't cover up the picture to 'stop them cheating'. The pictures are there for a reason. If they get stuck, encourage them to have a good look at the pictures, think about what's happened so far, take another look at the word and guess. Learning to guess is all part of the process.

Keep checking that your child has understood the story. 'Have you told dad what happens in your new reading book?' Getting him to tell the story in his own words will really help. And make sure your child understands that word he's just struggled to build. He might be able to work out that it says 'confused', but does he know what it means?

Don't keep him guessing for an age. If your child is really stuck and can't work a word out, help him to spell it out slowly and then say it faster together.

And don't pick him up after every mistake. Let him at least get to the end of the sentence before you point out an error. In time, he'll learn to pick up on his own mistakes and go back to correct them.

Reinforce the message that learning to read matters by getting your child used to reading in everyday life. Can he read the destination on the bus? Can he work out the sign above the shop? Can he read from the brochure about your holiday? Can he read a postcard from Grandma? Can he read just for the hell of it – knock, knock, a simple joke book usually does the trick.

Never forget that this is hard. Children need lots of praise and encouragement. If you feel your child is doing particularly well, you could even consider a reward. A book makes an excellent present!

What matters is that your child is interested, inspired and making progress. Don't panic if Emily down the road is on to *Harry Potter*. Be pleased for her. Be pleased for your own child.

The chances are that yours isn't the best or worst pupil in the class. And even if he's finding it painfully hard, keep reminding him of all the things he excels at. Everybody is good at something.

IMPROVING READERS

So, you go through all that and then what happens? Your child becomes a competent reader and you leave them to it.

A habit that's taken maybe nine years to establish disappears in a flurry of PlayStations or pop. Reading should never be something you only ever do because you have to. Reading should always be fun. But if you thought starting them reading was hard, keeping them reading might prove even harder.

To keep them going, you need to keep going, too. Take an interest in what they're reading, and make a real effort to ensure there's always something they'll want to read in the house.

Carry on reading with them, long after they are able to read for themselves. Don't stop the book at bedtime the day after they finish that first reading scheme. They will love you to go on reading to them for a long time yet. Share some of your old favourites and discover some new ones. Learn to share really good books together.

It's generally easier with girls. Girls who grow up with a love of storybooks will often continue to enjoy good stories thoughout their childhood and possibly all their lives. They'll enjoy talking to their friends about books they loved. They'll swap and share. They'll love books that tap into their emotions and teach them about friends and relationships from even the youngest age.

Boys can be trickier. Too many stop reading 'for pleasure' at a very young age. This is where you need to tap into your child's interests to keep them wanting more. It's no good making them read *The Secret Garden* because you loved it as a child if what they really want to read about is the solar system.

> **TOP TIP.** If your boy is a reluctant reader, go to the library and ask their advice – tap in to topics that suck your child in. And be sure to introduce a bit of variety. Don't make him read about the solar system *every* week.
>
> If you watched the football with him last night, show him the match report in today's paper. Get him to read it to you. It'll seem to him a grown-up, worthwhile thing to do.
>
> Double your money! Offer him a 'buy one, get one free' deal on his pocket money. If he normally gets £1, offer him £2 if he spends it on a book. And when he's read it, get him to lend it to a friend. He's more likely to keep reading if those all-important friends are reading, too.

Remember that boys generally need extra encouragement and there's a danger that they'll see reading as all a bit girlie unless they have male role models who show an interest in reading, too.

Get dad or grandad to read with them, let them see dad enjoying reading himself. Let dad be the one who takes him to the library sometimes. Let dad treat him to a book. Find time for them to read together.

Go with the flow. Whatever you think of Harry Potter, there's no denying that he's done more to get boys (and girls) reading than Robinson Crusoe ever could. Do all of that – *Harry Potter*, *Lord of the Rings*, whatever appeals. Get him going. He might not want to stop.

And never forget all that time you spent with Thomas the Tank Engine, stuck in the snow. If you could grit your teeth and bear it then, *Harry Potter* will be a breeze.

A GOOD READ

Recommended books for primary age children.

Key Stage 1, five to seven years

Bedford, D., *Shaggy Dog and the Terrible Itch*, Little Tiger Press, 2002

Blundell, T., *Beware of Girls*, Puffin Books, 2002

Chichester-Clark, E., *Where Are You, Blue Kangaroo?*, Picture Lions, 2001

Child, L., *I Am Not Sleepy and I Will Not Go to Bed*, Orchard Books, 2002

Dodds, D., *The Kettles Get New Clothes*, Walker Books, 2002

Dupasquier, P., *A Sunday with Grandpa*, Andersen Press, 2000

Grindley, S., *Mulberry out on the Town*, Hodder Children's Books, 2000

Horn, S., *Nobody, Him and Me*, Macmillan Children's Books, 2003

Lewis, K., *Little Baa*, Walker Books, 2004

MacDonald, A., *Snarlyhissopus*, Scholastic, 2003

Maddox, T., *Fergus to the Rescue*, Piccadilly Press, 2002

Mitton, T., *Down by the Cool of the Pool*, Orchard Books, 2002

Rosen, M., *Little Rabbit Foo Foo*, Walker Books, 2003

Whybrow, I., *Harry and the Bucketful of Dinosaurs*, Puffin Books, 2003

Wisdom, J., *Whatever Wanda Wanted*, Phyllis Fogelman Books, 2002

Woelfle, G., *Katje the Windmill Cat*, Walker Books, 2002

Wormell, C., *George and the Dragon*, Red Fox, 2003

Key Stage 2, seven to eleven years

For the lower age group in this category:

Anholt, L., *Old King Cole Played in Goal*, Orchard Books, 2003

Blake, J., *The Deadly Secret of Dorothy W.*, Hodder Children's Books, 2003

Cole, B., *Truelove*, Puffin Books, 2003

Crebbin, J., *Hal the Highwayman*, Walker Books, 2003

Grindley, S., *The Hare and the Tortoise*, Bloomsbury, 2000

Johnson, P., *Bug Brother*, Puffin Books, 2000

Markham, L., *Ghost Sister*, Egmont Books, 2003

McNaughton, C., *S.W.A.L.K.*, Andersen Press, 2002

Morpurgo, M., *The Last Wolf*, Doubleday, 2002

Rayner, S., *Breakout!*, Hodder Children's Books, 2002

Simon, F., *Horrid Henry's Stinkbomb*, Orion, 2002

Strong, J., *Krazy Kow Saves the World – Well Almost*, Puffin Books, 2002

Swindells, R., *Doodlebug Alley*, Mammoth, 2000

Whybrow, I., *A Footballer Called Flip*, Hodder Children's Books, 2000

Willis, J., *The Wind in the Wallows*, Red Fox, 2000

For the upper age group:

Blume, J., *Double Fudge*, Macmillan Children's Books, 2003

Booth, M., *Doctor Illuminatus*, Puffin Books, 2003

Briggs, R., *Ug*, Red Fox, 2002

Bunting, E., *The Summer of Riley*, Collins, 2002

Child, L., *Utterly Me, Clarice Bean*, Orchard Books, 2003

Cooper, L., *Demon Crossing*, Hodder Children's Books, 2002

Funke, C., *The Thief Lord*, Chicken House, 2002

Gleitzman, M., *Boy Overboard*, Puffin Books, 2003

Grindley, S., *Feather Wars*, Bloomsbury, 2003

Horowitz, A., *Point Blanc*, Walker Books, 2001

Kay, J., *Strawgirl*, Macmillan Children's Books, 2003

Pennac, D., *Dog*, Walker Books, 2002

Turnbull, A., *House of Ghosts*, Walker Books, 2001

Wilson, J., *Sleepovers*, Corgi Children's Books, 2002

WRITING

There's one foolproof way of gauging how far five-year-olds have developed their writing skills during their first term in Year One.

In December, you give them a sheet of paper and ask them to write down their Christmas wish list. Lo and behold, the children who have previously struggled to fill a couple of lines are soon asking for a second sheet so that nothing from the entire Argos toy collection could possibly be missed.

It's a handy reminder that, given the right topic, most children can be cajoled into putting their thoughts down on paper.

Many children are eager to write from a young age. Others are, to say the least, a little less keen. So, how do you get them started, and how do you spur them on when the novelty has worn off?

GETTING STARTED

Like all things grown-up, writing holds a great fascination for many young children. Not long after they start drawing vaguely recognisable pictures, they might well show an interest in having a go at writing.

A good starting place for any normal, self-centred three-year-old is his own name. Try showing your child how to write the first letter of his name. He might try to copy the shape you've drawn, or he might want to write over the top of a series of pencil dashes you've drawn for him.

Once he's mastered that all-important first letter, try moving him on to the others. Remember, only use a capital letter at the beginning of the name. It will be the lower-case, small letters that the child will need to master first.

From the moment you start, use any possible excuse to get your child practising. A little and often, as they say. If he paints a picture, can he put his name on the top? Can he sign Granny's birthday card? Can he make a name badge? Can he write his name in the front of a favourite book?

The more proficient children become, the more their confidence will grow and the more they'll want to learn. Don't underestimate the importance of leading by example. Every time your child sees you write a note, letter or list, he'll grasp the message that writing has a value.

Try writing a shopping list with him. You could write the word 'apple', then he could draw a picture of one. Perhaps he could trace over your pencil marks, or try writing the first letter. Then take the list with you and compare your writing with the word under the fruit on the supermarket shelf. Can he see that 'a' for apple? Can he tick it off on your list?

Any writing you can do together will reinforce the message that writing serves a purpose. If you've got 's' for sweets on that shopping list, you're definitely on a winner.

> **TOP TIP:** Let young children practise their writing with felt pens and big sheets of paper. It's so much easier to make your mark. The main aim at this stage is to get them used to making the shapes that form letters, so don't worry about untidy writing. Expect too much too soon and they might give up altogether.

EARLY WRITING SKILLS

Once children grasp that writing is just another way of telling some-body something, they'll usually want to learn more. They'll start to memorise how to write some simple words and they'll start to have a stab at writing words they don't know.

It's at this stage that your child's writing could well be somewhat tricky to decipher. Think of it as a text message and you might have more luck in working out what he's trying to say. Look at the letters he's written and think of the sounds. If he's written a complex word that makes phonetic sense – 'dynersor' for 'dinosaur' – rest assured that he's on the right track.

A young child's written work is often full of crossings out as they try different spellings. Don't worry about it. It's a sign that he's thinking about what he's doing and trying to get it right. He might like to have a piece of scrap paper to try out words before copying them into his notebook.

If your young child wants to write a story, have a go at writing it together. He'll learn from watching you write. He might like to give you a bit of advice on your spelling as you go along. And there could be some words he can write himself.

Talk to him about tenses so that he starts to get used to those changing verbs. And think about punctuation. Your child will need to know about full stops and question marks a lot sooner than you think.

ENCOURAGING A RELUCTANT WRITER

Some children can't get enough of writing. For others – and probably most – the literacy hour is more than ample, thank you very much.

Cajoling most children to read is a piece of cake compared with persuading them to write at home. So what do you do to make writing something they actually want to do? Here are some tips you could try:

- **Competitions:** Most children love competitions, particularly if the prize is something they really want to win. It doesn't have to be a grand literary contest. Even if they're only filling in their name and address on a competition form in the hopes of winning a bike, it's all writing and it all hammers home the message that writing has a value.
- **Autobiographies:** Can your child write his own life story? Select some baby pictures, toddler pictures, and 'first day at school' pictures then stick them in his own photograph album. What can you tell him that he can record about the day he was born? Can he write a caption to go with that picture from his first summer holiday with his chocolate ice cream all down daddy's shirt? A nice little project and a lovely keepsake.
- **Kids' Clubs:** Join a club that taps into your child's interest. Many of the clubs for children – the Lego club, for instance – are free and will encourage both reading and writing.
- **Puzzles:** Does granny like her crosswords? Would she sit with her grandson and fill in a child's crossword book?
- **Secret messages:** Go back to your own childhood with invisible ink. Would-be Action Men will love it.
- **Diaries:** Could your child keep a diary under lock and key? Could he fill in all those questions about favourite colours and favourite pop stars?
- **Cards and thank-you letters:** Encourage your child to design birthday cards for his friends. Get him to write his own party invitations. And how much pleasure will he get from writing all those thank-you letters – well, yes, that's stretching the point, but you get the idea.
- **Scrapbooks:** These are a great way to remind you of a holiday. Stick in that scorecard and encourage your child to write the story

of the day he beat his dad at crazy golf. Could he take his own photographs to use as illustrations?

- **E-mails:** You don't have to have a pen in your hand to write. Writing on a computer still involves spelling and punctuation. E-mail a friend, e-mail a club, e-mail a child in another country and find a pen friend.
- **Write to someone important:** Write to the Prime Minister, the Queen, the Mayor, the chairman of Manchester United about something that matters to your child. The chances are he'll get a reply on highly impressive notepaper. Great for taking in and showing off to teacher.
- **Write to your local newspaper:** Write about the traffic problems at your school, the state of your local park, a thank-you letter drawing attention to someone who did something special. No paper worth its salt could possibly resist taking a photograph of your child and making them headline news.
- **Write your own newspaper:** Can your child pretend to be an ace reporter and write in newspaper style? Could he write a sports report of the football match he's just watched?
- **Use your imagination:** Are there fairies at the bottom of your garden? Find out by leaving hidden letters and seeing if the fairies write back!

Don't forget that novelty may well be the key to keeping children's interest. There are lots of cheap and cheerful pens and pencils on the market that will intrigue even the most reluctant writer. Try gel pens, Spiderman pens, colour-change pens, different pencils, different rubbers. Write with white on black paper, or write in glue and cover it with glitter. Remember, children have so much of writing with pencil on white paper at school that that may well be the last thing they want to do at home.

SPELLING

Lots of children find spelling tough. Don't be discouraged if yours is among them.

Your child needs lots of encouragement to persevere with learning spellings. It's important that you support him. Regaling him with tales of your own spelling disasters really won't help. He needs to know that being able to spell matters, and he needs to hear it from you.

That said, don't knock the confidence of a new writer by picking him up on every spelling mistake he makes. Tactfully point out the mistakes you feel he should reasonably have avoided. So, for instance, a child who is finding spelling hard should still be able to work out how to write 'it'. A more capable child should be able to remember 'because' if it was part of last week's spelling test.

Playing games is a good way to get children used to spelling patterns. Tell them about the 'magic e' that turns 'tap' into 'tape' and 'hop' into 'hope'.

Encourage your child to do word puzzles. Here's your chance to recruit Granny again for word searches and anagrams. By rearranging the letters, how many other words can he make out of his own name?

Try him with lists of words to put in alphabetical order. Then make it tougher still by seeing if he can do the same task with the second letter in the word – cat, cot, cut.

Keep magnetic letters at child-level on the fridge door. Can he write a different daily message for dad? Can it not contain the word 'poo' *every* night?

Try to keep the whole thing light and fun. If every other word in your child's diary is 'cool', learn to live with it. What you're teaching is the fun side of writing and communicating. It isn't the literacy hour re-visited.

TOP TIP. As soon as your child is reading and writing, buy a children's dictionary to have on hand at home. It will get him used to the way dictionaries work, build his skills at finding words, and improve his vocabulary. But don't expect a young child to master it straight away. He'll need help in looking up words and guessing how a word might start.

MATHS

Come on, now. No shirking at the back. Just because this is the bit about maths, you're not allowed to skip to the next chapter.

What is it about maths, anyway? Why is it that a parent who would rather die than admit they found reading difficult at school will happily confess to being brain-dead when it comes to numbers?

'I was rubbish at maths at school,' they say. 'Still am. Can't add up to save my life. My little girl takes after me. Thinks take-aways are something to do with fish and chips. Ha-ha!' Oh, how we all laugh.

But how many of us remember it being funny at the time? How many of us remember the blind panic of the Monday morning maths test when the best we could hope for was a miracle to make the random numbers we chose as answers somehow fit the questions?

On the face of it, today's children can hardly be considered better off. They have a daily numeracy lesson devoted to boosting their maths skills. But if that sounds like hell to you, you may well find that your child surprises you by actually quite enjoying it.

One of the reasons is that over the last three years or so, there has been a revolution in the way maths is taught. And many of those who teach it feel it's been a change for the better.

There's generally much more emphasis now on mental arithmetic, getting children used to doing calculations without forever having a pen in one hand and a calculator in the other. Often the first question a teacher will ask is: can you do this in your head? And if they can, they do.

The whole approach is more logical, the goal to get children understanding numbers, not just putting them through the tedious process of rote learning.

Information technology is also playing a part in encouraging children to enjoy maths. The whole thing is much more visual, the entire experience much less painful. How much more enjoyable to pretend to be slicing up a pizza and calculating the bills in your pizzeria than drawing pie charts with a compass and, only if the teacher was feeling extraordinarily generous, getting to colour the biggest segment pink.

And, because it's fun, many children who would have been turned off by the old methods have come to love maths. They're interested, lively, and really involved in their learning. The teacher is no longer flogging a dead horse, the children are no longer dreading their maths lessons, and it all adds up to a better education.

AS A PARENT, WHAT CAN I DO?

Well, an excellent first step would be to stop endlessly going on about how bad you are at maths! It only gives your child an excuse to give up on the subject the way many of us did.

The next step would be to find out what teaching methods are being used in your child's school. This really is one instance where winging it is not a good option.

Trying to help your child with his homework by showing him methods you were taught 25 years ago won't help anyone. You'll confuse him and you'll almost certainly confuse yourself.

Ask the teacher to show you what methods they are using in class. You might even want to invest in one of those 'How to revise in maths' books, though not, for goodness' sake, to ply your child with endless additional homework. Take a sneaky look through it yourself. You might be amazed by what you pick up. You might even have to stop telling everyone just how bad at maths you are – or thought you were.

Do children bother learning their times tables any more? They certainly do. The target is that every child will know up to their ten times table by the time they're ten years old. You can help by practising at home from around the time your child moves into the juniors.

Try the easy ones first – two, three, five and ten are a good starting point – and it'll help if you join in saying them aloud with your child at first (assuming you can remember them yourself).

The ultimate aim is that children will know them inside out, not just knowing that two fives are ten, but that five twos are ten just the same.

And another tip – go metric. Oh, go on, it's easier. How many of us would even contemplate going back to pounds, shillings and pence with all that appalling adding up in twelves? So why is it that we persist in sticking with a weights and measures system so complicated that most of us can't remember the rules anyway? Not convinced? OK, how many inches in a mile? Now try asking your ten-year-old how many centimetres in a kilometre. We rest our case.

MAKING MATHS FUN

Even the youngest children enjoy playing games with numbers. From the first time you discard your favourite CD and sing along to 'Five Little Speckled Frogs' in the car instead, the great maths adventure has begun.

And because numbers are all around us, a quick maths lesson need never be far away. With the emphasis now so much on mental arithmetic, there's a lot you can do to get your child used to flashing numbers through his head.

- **At the shops:** Go to a proper fruit and veg shop and let your child do the weighing. Go to the corner shop and buy three or four items.

Can he calculate the cost? Can he work out what money he needs from your purse to pay for them? How much change will he get back?

- **At the café:** If the cake costs £1.20 a slice and cuts into eight slices, how much will the café make on the whole cake?
- **In a traffic jam:** Get him to add up all the numbers on the number plate of the car in front. Which is the biggest number? Which is the smallest? An older child might be able to multiply the last two numbers by the first.

At some stage, you might want to start giving your primary-age child pocket money. It needn't be much, but it will start to get him used to handling money. And it leads to further questions. How many weeks before he can afford that new CD? What if he can find it somewhere at 20% discount – how much would it cost then?

Trick your child into doing maths by targeting something enjoyable. You may have a girl who would love a pink diary with a lock and key. Could she record her school timetable in it? If she gets home at 3.30 p.m., how many hours is it to bedtime? How many weeks to her birthday? How many weeks since she was born? How many days?

If you've a hyper-competitive boy, turn mental arithmetic into a competition. Most boys love a challenge. How fast can he count to 200 in tens? How fast can he do it backwards? Can he do it with fives? Can he be even faster next time? Time him on your watch or, better still, buy a cheap stopwatch for that professional quizmaster feel. Remember, it's supposed to be fun. You are not Anne Robinson.

Make time to play board games. Even young children will have a stab at dominoes or snakes and ladders. And an older child will relish something like Junior Monopoly with the added challenge of money to count and the possible bonus of giving him that early thirst for financial supremacy.

But don't get carried away. Numbers *are* everywhere, but it doesn't mean maths lessons have to be everywhere all the time, too. It's great to go to the supermarket and get them to count the oranges and it's good to add up number plates on the way. But, you know, sometimes it's nice to just do the shopping and sing along to 'Reach for the Stars' at volume nine on the way back. Maths should be fun, not a constant chore.

14 MOVING INTO THE JUNIORS

Moving into the juniors is the next milestone and it creeps up on you before you know it. One minute you're there weeping at the school gates having waved off a four-year-old in a huge school sweatshirt, the next you've got a gap-toothed seven-year-old with gangly legs sticking out of half-mast trousers, all ready for the big move up.

It's goodbye to the toys, to the unforgettable infant teachers, to friends in the next class down, to lunchtime videos on bitterly cold days, to younger siblings, and farewell to the kudos of being the top infants, hero-worshipped by the four-year-olds and brimming with self-confidence.

Gone forever is the child you sent in, the one who was terrified of the baddie at his first school pantomime, who hardly spoke for the first month, who was dead on his feet by half-term.

This child can read and write, has completed his first big tests without either of you having a nervous breakdown, and has stood up in front of the whole school to say: 'Follow the star,' as the second shepherd in the Christmas nativity.

Now, it's back to square one. Suddenly, he's the tiddler again, the smallest in the juniors, trying to keep up with a whole new playground etiquette overseen by lads as tall as the teachers and arguably with more influence than some of the staff.

For many children, of course, it means a move to a new school as they leave the comfort blanket of the infants behind. Some go to a separate junior school until they're eleven. In some areas, they move to a middle school until they're thirteen or fourteen. For the rest, it might be no more than a move across a corridor in their primary school. But for all children it's still a big leap.

They can expect to find their days much more structured to tie in with the national curriculum. They might well also find themselves in a noticeably larger class. Class sizes in the infants are strictly limited to a maximum of thirty, but there's no limit yet on numbers in the juniors. And, while there are only so many children one teacher can teach, it's not uncommon for numbers to rise above that previous thirty limit.

They're also likely to face a marked increase in homework. Schools vary, but the benchmark is around half-an-hour a day throughout the juniors. That's quite some commitment for a seven-year-old who might still have no more than four hours between getting home and going to bed.

And, as parents, don't expect the easy ride you had in the infants. Homework is likely to become more taxing all round as children move on to more involved work – researching, perhaps, a history project to tie in with their topic.

A whole new vocabulary starts to sneak into the timetable as children start to recognise the subjects they're studying. So science becomes science and not just a topic on dinosaurs.

Teachers are allowed some flexibility, but are expected to spend an allocated amount of time on certain subjects.

The classrooms themselves take on a much more grown-up look. The colourful artwork is still there, but is now scattered among maps of Britain and essays on the Romans.

Classes are still largely mixed, but children tend to work in groups according to ability, so don't be too alarmed if your child's class seems particularly big. The chances are that other qualified teachers will filter off children at various stages in the day for group work.

Even PE is likely to become much more structured. Teachers will probably introduce more team games as what was previously an energy-burning romp around the hall in vest and knickers turns into something much more serious. Fathers take note. Here at last is the perfect excuse to buy your lad his first pair of football boots.

YES, BUT IS IT FUN?

More structure, more subjects, more timetables – it doesn't exactly sound a bundle of laughs, does it?

But those in the know, teachers with many years' experience behind them, seem largely agreed that today's schoolchildren have a much better time than most of us enjoyed.

The child is very much at the centre of every decision taken in primary schools. The best teachers have a firm understanding of how children react and where they're coming from. They make it their business to stay on the children's wavelength. They know that if David Beckham scores a hat trick for England they can expect to walk into a pretty lively class the next morning.

What they know doesn't work is to sit children in ranks of desks and talk at them, all day every day, filling their minds with facts that mean nothing to them now and probably never will. Their role is no longer as dictator. What they want to do is fire the children up, get them to enjoy learning, give them a lifelong thirst for knowledge.

And they recognise the need to keep parents on board as their children start to grow into the citizens of the future. The older children get, the more important the role of parents in shaping their attitudes, values, and view of the world. Schools can only do so much. Rest assured that as your child moves through the juniors and grows more independent, his teachers are going to need your help now as much as ever.

> There's a saying, 'Children aren't vessels to be filled, they're candles to be lit.' Instead of pouring in fact after fact after fact, you have to light their enthusiasm. We want them to become independent learners who value learning for its own sake. That applies equally to the very intelligent children and the less able.
>
> *A deputy head*

PEER PRESSURE

Any parent who has sent a child to school will tell you that, from the moment their child walks through the door, they have a rival for the child's affections.

Young children almost universally hero-worship their teacher. For a week or two, this strikes you as ideal.

'What's your new teacher like?' everyone asks your child.

'Nice,' he says, a little coyly, like an adult admitting to a new infatuation.

After a while, it starts to become a little wearing.

'Miss Brown says we don't have to wear our scarves.'

'Miss Brown says not to bring crisps because they're bad for you.'

'Miss Brown doesn't say "bath", she says "barth".'

'Miss Brown doesn't read like that, she teaches me the right way.'

Miss Brown, Miss Brown, soon just the name starts to have the same effect as fingernails scratched down a blackboard.

However much it irks to have this new and much-loved authority figure in your child's life, the smart parent quickly turns the situation to their advantage.

'Miss Brown says you must always be in bed by 7.30 p.m.'

'Miss Brown says you must always learn your spellings.'

'Miss Brown says you must keep your room tidy, be polite at all times, and grow to love sprouts.'

Some teachers openly admit that one of the great attractions of teaching infants is that wide-eyed, open-mouthed adulation that comes as standard with most little children. Away from mum all day, often for the first time, they latch on to this mother or father substitute like orphaned ducklings, following the teacher's lead, hanging on to their every word. It's a position of unquestioning authority few parents ever enjoy!

And then, as these things do, it all goes wrong. Children start to grow up and suddenly realise that not all teachers are God.

At some point, particularly towards the end of primary school, friends begin to take the place of teachers, parents, brothers and sisters as a key influence in a child's life. Whatever *they* wear, whatever *they* do, is now what your child wants most in all the world. The more popular the child, the greater their influence. And girls are by far the worst.

So what do you do when your once-compliant child turns into a nine-year-old adolescent who can no longer see the point in school? Well, you certainly need to get it right now because otherwise it's going to be a long hard road between here and university.

A common mistake is to come down like a ton of bricks on this nine-year-old girl who thinks she's the new Britney Spears. Be warned. Sever lines of communication now and you might never get them back.

Minimise the opportunities for her to roll her eyes and stomp off to her bedroom by negotiating your way out of trouble. Instead of a conversation starting and ending with: 'No, you're definitely not having your ears pierced and that's my last word on the subject,' try to get her to see your point of view.

Sit down and discuss it rationally. Explain what could go wrong, what a pain it could be, having to tape up earrings for PE, what a danger in a busy playground. See if you can reach a compromise.

You may as well get used to it. It's going to be all compromise from now on. Much as you might resent your child being catapulted into adulthood before she's had a chance to outgrow Barbie, the fact remains that today's children are under enormous pressure to grow up too soon.

If you rubbish her friends, her dress sense, her taste in music, you run the risk that she'll start to reject you.

That doesn't mean you have to say yes when she wants you to spend an impossible amount of money on designer gear that makes her look like an adult. You'll do her no favours if you set her on the slippery slope to want, want, want at such a young age.

But you will have to accept that, like it or not, her friends are now hugely important to her. They give her a group identity, teach her a new vocabulary (oh, joy), introduce her to music that'll drive you crazy, and phone her twice a night even though they've spent all day together.

What's more, these exciting new friends are allowed to watch *EastEnders*, stay up late, and read magazines that mention sex. No wonder they're more interesting than you.

But before you reject them as wholly unsuitable company for the daughter you wish you still had, try to get to know them. Help your daughter negotiate the confusing maze of this much-too-early growing up. Help her to find a way to fit in and be liked at school and at home. She needs to be happy in both places – she needs not necessarily to hero-worship her teacher, but at least to respect her.

And from now on, she's going to need all the encouragement you can give to keep her school and home life on track.

15 THE NATIONAL CURRICULUM: KEY STAGE 2

After the hurdle of those first SATs tests comes Key Stage 2 for children aged seven to eleven.

All state schools in England have to teach English, maths, science, design and technology, information and communication technology, history, geography, art and design, music, physical education and religious education. Each school can organise the teaching as it thinks best and not every subject is taught in separate lessons.

ENGLISH

By the start of Key Stage 2, children should have the basic skills they need to be able to put their thoughts into writing much more easily. They read not only to find out facts, but for fun, and they start to express an opinion about what they read.

Children are taught, almost always during a daily literacy hour:

- **Speaking and listening:** Great store is placed on listening skills. Children are taught to listen carefully and pick out the key facts. They are encouraged to ask questions and make comments. They write scripts or improvise plays and evaluate their own performance. They are taught about how language changes in different situations, and between speech and writing.
- **Reading:** Children read broadly and use their skills to work out the meaning. They improve at reading long and difficult texts on their own, and discuss the meaning of both fiction and non-fiction with others.
- **Writing:** Children write in a range of ways. They explore feelings, persuade, review and comment. They plan and check their work, improving punctuation, spelling and grammar. They produce legible, joined-up writing.

TARGETS

By the end of Year Six most children should be able to:

- **Speaking and listening:** Listen to presentations and discussions and talk about what they have heard. Develop and shape ideas and stories using language imaginatively. Use some of the features of formal English when appropriate.
- **Reading:** Understand important ideas, events and characters. Read between the lines. Give ideas about a text and refer back to it to support their view. Use different ways to find information in print and on screen.
- **Writing:** Write in a lively, thoughtful way in a range of forms, using words adventurously and for effect. Organise ideas to draw them to the reader's attention. Spell accurately, most of the time. Use punctuation to make meaning clear. Write legibly and fluently in joined-up writing.

MATHEMATICS

In Key Stage 2 children learn how to use maths. They decide how to go about tackling problems and then record what they do using mathematical language, symbols and diagrams. They use a calculator to solve certain sorts of problems, but are usually expected to do the maths in their heads or on paper.

Children are taught, almost always during a daily maths lesson:

- **Number:** Numbers and the number system, calculations and problem solving.
- **Shape, space and measures:** Including two-dimensional and three-dimensional shapes, position, movement and measurement.
- **Handling data:** Working out which questions can be answered by collecting data, organising it, putting it into graphs and diagrams, and working out how it provides the answer to the original question.

TARGETS

By the end of Year Six most children are expected to be able to:

- **Using and applying maths:** Tackle a problem using different approaches. Apply maths to practical problems. Present their results clearly.
- **Number:** Multiply and divide decimals by 10 or 100, and whole numbers by 1,000 in their heads. Put in order a set of numbers with up to three decimal places. Work with decimals to add and subtract. Reduce a fraction to its simplest form. Work out fractions of numbers or quantities. Grasp that a percentage is the number of parts in every hundred, and work out simple percentages. Solve problems involving ratio and proportion. Know all the times tables

and use them to divide and multiply. Use +, −, ÷ and × to solve problems given in words which could be about numbers or measures. Use paper and pencil methods of multiplying and dividing for harder calculations.

- **Shape, space and measure:** Use a protractor to measure angles. Calculate the perimeter and areas of shapes that can be split into rectangles. Read and plot co-ordinates in all four quadrants. Interpret numbers accurately on a range of measuring instruments. Tell the time and solve problems on a 12-hour or 24-hour clock.
- **Handling data:** Solve a problem by collecting and using information in tables, graphs and charts.

SCIENCE

This subject revolves around scientific enquiry, that leap that children are encouraged to take to find out more about the world around them.

The teacher or the children themselves ask questions, and then the children work together to find the answers. They might record data, look for patterns in it, use reference books and computer sources, and will write and draw (sometimes on computers) what they discover. Then they will think about what they did and whether they went about answering the questions in the most sensible way.

Children look at and explore:

- **Life processes and living things:** They will learn about their own bodies, such as the need for healthy food and exercise. They will look at the purpose of roots and flowers in plants, how animals and plants are classified, and their habitats.
- **Materials and their properties:** Including how they can be used, how they change, and how some can be mixed and separated.
- **Physical processes:** Including electric circuits, magnets, the forces of gravity and friction, and how light and sound travel. They also learn some of the basics about the sun, earth and moon.

TARGETS

By the end of Year Six most children should be able to:

- **Scientific enquiry:** Recognise that scientific ideas are based on evidence. Suggest practical ways to answer scientific questions. Set up tests, make a series of observations or measurements, and record them on tables, charts and graphs. Predict the outcome.
- **Life processes and living things:** Name major body organs and

know where they are. Name parts of plants. Identify and group animals and plants. Explain their knowledge of the food chain.

- **Materials and their properties**: Classify materials by their properties. Describe ways of separating substances. Use scientific names for some changes, such as 'evaporation'. Use knowledge about which changes can or cannot be reversed (such as turning ice back to water) to predict whether other changes can be reversed.
- **Physical processes:** Connect, make changes to and draw diagrams of simple electrical circuits. Describe what happens to light and sound when we see and hear. Describe the appearance of the sun, earth and moon and how their positions change. Generalise about forces: for example, magnets attract.

DESIGN AND TECHNOLOGY

Children are taught to look at products to see how they work, how they are used, and what people think of them. They practise practical tasks, such as cutting and joining. They use the skills they have learned to design and create their own products, and then put what they made to the test.

TARGETS

By the end of Year Six most children should have a range of design and technology skills including: finding out how people use different products and using that information to think up improvements; explaining their design ideas with step-by-step plans; putting together materials; and working with a broad range of tools, including computers.

INFORMATION AND COMMUNICATION TECHNOLOGY

A subject taught not just for school, but for life. Children use a range of ICT tools and information sources to support their work in other subjects. They are taught that information must be accurate and relevant, which means filtering good information from bad, particularly from the Internet. They also learn to look at and compare the ways ICT is used both in school and in the world outside.

TARGETS

Skills acquired by most children by the end of Year Six should include: using ICT to present information and share ideas, including using e-mail; checking the reliability of information; writing and testing simple computer programs to control and monitor events, such as switching on a light bulb at dusk; and using simulation software to test theories.

Other subjects covered include:

HISTORY

Local, British, European and international history are all covered. Children learn about the Romans, Anglo-Saxons and Vikings in Britain; Britain and the wider world in Tudor times; either Victorian Britain or Britain since 1930; the ancient Greeks; and one from a list of past societies.

As well as learning about kings, queens and famous people, they learn to look at history from different viewpoints, such as political, social and religious.

GEOGRAPHY

Children use maps, atlases and plans to study all sorts of places: local, regional and national. They learn about important places and environments in the world. And they look at the environment on their doorstep by, for instance, studying a local stream or looking at the different types of shops in their town centre. The ways people and the environment affect each other are also part of their studies.

ART AND DESIGN

Children develop and explore their ideas, mixing different materials and techniques. They review their own work and that of others, and look at the roles of artists, craftspeople and designers in different times and cultures.

MUSIC

Children sing and play musical instruments. They learn how to express their ideas and feelings through their own music. And they are introduced to many different types of music.

PHYSICAL EDUCATION

The aim, at least, is that this is where children learn the message that will stay with them for life – that keeping fit can be fun. They do it through dance, games (some of which they invent themselves), gymnastics, swimming, athletics and outdoor activities. They also start to play adapted versions of adult sports like netball and cricket.

The target for most schools is to have children exercising, both in PE lessons and out-of-hours sports, for about two hours a week.

RELIGIOUS EDUCATION

Children learn about the main religions in the country, particularly Christianity. The aim is that they will come to respect the beliefs and practices of others as well as discovering more about their own.

Schools have to teach religious education, but there is no national pro-gramme of study. Children are encouraged to explore what they believe, ask deeper questions, and look at what is considered to be right and wrong.

PERSONAL, SOCIAL AND HEALTH EDUCATION, AND CITIZENSHIP

Not a compulsory subject, but one which schools are encouraged to introduce. The aim is to help children grow in confidence and maturity, and to help plan their own future goals. They are also taught social skills, such as how the choices they make affect others, and how to get on with other social groups.

Sex and relationship education

Because opinions are so varied on sex education, your child's school has to provide a written statement about its policy. It will say whether sex and relationship education will be taught and, if so, what it will amount to, and from what age it will be taught.

Children will learn about the main stages of the human life cycle from their science lessons by the time they leave primary school. Many schools also choose to look at the emotions and morality surrounding sexual relationships. You can opt to take your child out of these lessons, but not from the relevant science lessons.

Don't worry if your child's school doesn't seem to be teaching all these subjects. Schools are expected to do literacy and maths lessons daily, and PE weekly, but how they cover the rest of the curriculum is up to individual schools. Some subjects might be taught in blocks, and some might be taught under a different name. Your child will, for instance, be studying geography when he does a lesson looking at where he and his classmates were born – he will probably be blissfully unaware that he's just sat through his first geography lesson.

16 HELPING YOUR CHILD'S SCHOOL

However much time or money you have to spare, there are several ways you can help your child's school.

HELPING IN SCHOOLS

With ever-increasing calls on a teacher's time in the classroom, any help they can recruit from other adults is generally welcome.

Some of the additional help they need comes from paid teaching assistants. Their key role enables the teacher to concentrate on a small group of children at a time, perhaps reading, perhaps doing assessments, without the constant interruptions that inevitably break into any primary school class.

The assistant often has the unenviable task of helping other children with their own tasks, maintaining order, and dealing with all those requests for trips to the toilet from children who couldn't quite bring themselves to sacrifice two minutes of playtime for something as trivial as the loo.

But, in addition to the assistants they can afford to employ, most schools rarely turn away an offer of extra help. Parents – both mums and dads – who volunteer maybe a couple of hours a week to help in schools are generally welcomed with open arms.

Not only do they help to encourage the children's learning and take some of the pressure off the teacher, they also go away with a crystal-clear vision of how today's children are taught and a real insight into how to help their own child progress.

So, all mutually beneficial and totally problem-free then? Well, not quite. There can be problems on both sides unless both school and parent pull together to make the system work.

Without help and encouragement, it would, after all, be a pretty confident parent who put themselves forward. A common complaint among parent volunteers is that initially they felt totally out of their depth, unable to make any kind of useful judgment or feel that they were being a genuine help when plunged into an education system they knew nothing about.

And teachers can find themselves in an equally awkward situation. How do you tell somebody that they are making mistakes when they are voluntarily sacrificing their free time to help?

Perhaps teachers should spare their own blushes and pin up the following guide to give their volunteers a subtle nudge in the right direction.

THE PARENT HELPERS FROM HELL

They come in various guises:

1. **The Mother Hen:** The worst volunteers are those who don't know the difference between being a parent and being a parent helper. They sit the children on their knees and call them 'honey' or 'love' or 'petal'. They talk to them as they would if they were round at their house for tea. They do that whole surrogate mother 'Oh, are you tired, tuppence?' thing – and then two hours later breeze out leaving the teacher to pick up the pieces.
2. **The Bossy Boots:** Then there are the ones who get a sniff of the classroom chalk and go power crazy. They turn into the teacher they used to hate when they were at school. Thank goodness for the abolition of the cane.
3. **The Infiltrator:** They are there for one thing and one thing only – to spy on the school. These are the volunteers who are convinced that their child isn't being taught properly. They grudgingly give up their time 'to keep an eye on the teacher'. Their interest in helping anyone but themselves is minuscule.
4. **The Soft Touch:** They let the children rule the roost. Barely have they started the maths exercise before one of the children asks when she can next come to their house for tea and from then on the lesson degenerates into a discussion of the relative merits of chicken nuggets over fish fingers. Either that or the helper, unable to stick to the job in hand, gives up and lets the children do the same. 'I think this is a bit hard for you. Shall we play Lego instead?' Often, they do the work for the children, not least by commandeering the paintbrush in art.

5. **The Gossip:** Five minutes after leaving the classroom, they're holding a mothers' meeting at the school gates to report on everything they've seen. 'Ooh, that Thomas, he's a right monkey,' they tell the other parents. Or, worse still: 'Your Emma's rubbish at maths. You need to spend more time on her numbers. I hope you don't mind me saying...'

So, that's how not to do it. Now for how to do it well.

GOOD PARENT VOLUNTEERS

Any parent will be a godsend to the teacher if they:

1. **Take a professional attitude to their role:** They know the difference between talking to children and nattering as though they were having a picnic in the park. They learn to follow the teacher's lead, talking to the children kindly, but taking a firm, more formal approach that keeps the children busy and the lesson on track.
2. **Resist the urge to be too tactile:** They recognise that their role is to be surrogate teacher, not surrogate mum.
3. **Develop a teacher's sixth sense:** As an extra pair of eyes and ears, they're constantly on the lookout for children showing signs of needing help with their work. They don't see themselves as there only to monitor potential trouble.
4. **Act on their own initiative:** A volunteer who runs to the teacher for help every five minutes is scarily close to being an extra pupil. By using their own judgment – without veering away completely from the task they were set – they leave the teacher free to work with her own group. And while the volunteers might not get it right every time, it's a fair bet that neither does the teacher.
5. **Bring their own talents into the classroom:** Volunteers with the confidence to use their own strengths in school can be a huge asset. Some are exceptionally good at art and creating classroom displays, some excel at imaginative play, some are musicians, sportsmen, actors. And some even bring the day job along with them. Firefighters have been known to turn up with the occasional fire engine. Imagine what that does for their child's street cred.
6. **Can be dads!** Primary schools are generally so top heavy with women teachers that male role models are like gold dust. In modern times when so many children are growing up without fathers at home, schools are delighted to see more dads getting involved. Just being there, showing an interest, demonstrates to boys in particular that conscientious learning isn't just for girls.

THE BENEFICIAL EFFECTS OF PARENT HELPERS

Many schools report that just the fact that an extra adult is in the class-room seems to have a positive effect on the children. The more adults there are encouraging their studies, the more likely they are to knuck-le down.

And the broader the range, the better. Parents from ethnic minori-ties, for instance, can have a particularly strong influence. Teachers would generally be delighted to welcome a volunteer who could demonstrate ethnic cooking or perhaps show the children how to drape a sari. Their presence in the class alone would speak volumes to the children about how much education is valued by all sections of the community.

If you plan to volunteer your time, talk to the school about their policy towards parent volunteers. Most will be only too pleased to have you on board, but attitudes still vary from school to school and from teacher to teacher.

Many have come to appreciate the important work parents play in the classroom and give them a proper role to play.

Others are still uncomfortable about having parents in the classroom. Some feel that too many adults in a class at any one time can be dis-ruptive and confusing for the children. And there are those who still see parents as spies in the camp, hearing and seeing all they do.

Some schools get round a few of the potential problems by insisting that no parent is allowed to volunteer for their own child's class. That way there's less danger of school-gate gossip and less incentive for the parent who's only there to check on their own child's progress.

It's also common practice to ask parents to undergo a criminal records bureau check. Don't take it personally! Schools have an obvious responsibility to ensure that adults invited into schools are safe to be around children.

So, yes, volunteering to help in schools might be more complex than you thought. But the fact that schools are largely keen to give parents a more challenging role has to be a good thing.

Forget the potential problems – the potential gains on both sides are enormous. The best volunteers learn as much as the children do. They get a clear insight into how teachers teach and a real opportunity to kick-start their own child's learning.

If you're interested in becoming a volunteer, you might want to think about taking a part-time course on helping in schools. One avenue is the Workers' Educational Association, which runs particularly good courses of this nature. To find out more, contact the WEA at www.wea.org.uk or through their local district office, which should be listed in the phone book.

Volunteering to go into schools may even bring more benefits than you think. Many are the parents who went into school as a volunteer and proved so invaluable that their experience ultimately clinched them a job in education. Well, you never know.

> It's really interesting to see what happens in school. My son is in reception and I was quite shocked to see the level of the things they do. I've got a lot out of it. I understand a lot more about how school works now.
>
> My son really looks forward to me going in. I was in the other day when he did something he was really proud of and he just turned to me and beamed. It was lovely.
>
> *The mother of a five-year-old*

SCHOOL GOVERNORS

Becoming a school governor is not for the faint-hearted. Governors play a crucial role in helping to determine how their school is run. It's serious stuff and certainly not the kind of work you should consider just because it's another of those things that look good on a CV.

Every state school in England has a number of parent governors who work on the governing body alongside some of the school staff and representatives from the Local Education Authority.

If as a parent you'd like to become more involved in the running of your school, have a word with the head teacher about the possibility of becoming a governor. It may well be that you will have to stand for election when a vacancy arises and put your case in writing to help parents make their choice. You could well be up against stiff competition from other well-meaning parents, so think carefully about how you want to sell yourself. You may want to write something about your career, any relevant management experience you may have, details of your family, what you've already done to support the school, and what you could offer for the future.

If your bid for election is successful, you can expect to go through a nationally designed induction process outlining your roles and responsibilities. You may also have the opportunity to attend other training events organised by the Local Education Authority and other bodies.

WHAT IS THE ROLE OF GOVERNORS?

Governors are volunteers who help the head set the strategic direction for the school. Working with the head, they steer the school's course for the future, and decide how to spend its budget. They also work together in a range of key areas such as setting policies and performance targets.

They look at the big picture: monitoring the impact of their policies on the school, responding to recommendations following school inspections, hearing appeals from pupils and staff, and looking into complaints.

They also play a key role as intermediaries between the school and parents. It's often through the governors' reports that parents find out about the school's achievements.

What they also bring to schools is experience of the world outside. The skills and knowledge they have gleaned, whether from their working lives or through simply being parents, can be immensely helpful. Although they are expected to respect the position of the head teacher – who is, after all, a professional school leader – they are not expected to follow blindly everything he or she recommends. Good governors can and do ask probing questions.

WHAT NO ONE TELLS YOU ABOUT BEING A PARENT GOVERNOR

In theory, governors spend about six hours each month attending meetings and doing other work to help develop the school.

What comes on top is the amount of time you might be harangued in the school playground over the colour of the school uniform, or a dispute between pupils, or the lateness of the school bus.

It will be a minor miracle if you're not dragged into that old chestnut – the school-run parking headache, which has plagued school managers since time immemorial. The walk-to-school brigade will want you to ban cars within a three-mile radius, the drivers won't be happy until you've found them a parking space in the foyer. It's no-win all the way.

Like most voluntary public service, there are times when being a school governor will seem a thankless task. You can be as conscientious as you like all year, but the chances of needing more than a dozen seats when the governing body presents its annual report to parents are not high.

As for the reaction of the other parents, half won't have a clue who you are and a good proportion of the rest will assume you're either pushy or in it for what you can get.

SO, IS IT WORTH IT?

Absolutely. It is not an exaggeration to say that governors make a difference to children's futures. By helping to steer a school in the right direction, they help to improve the education not only of today's children but of those who follow them.

Governors play a key role in bringing the community into the school and the school into the community. They are not afraid to take on real responsibilities and share the head's burden. They put themselves forward because they care about the children and care about the school.

Never let the cynics put you off. Good schools need good governors. It's as simple as that.

THE PTA

To all but the most confident parent, there's something slightly intimidating about volunteering for the PTA.

Most schools have some kind of parent–teacher association, run ostensibly as a liaison group between the two. In reality, most spend their time fundraising. The days of the great British jumble sale live on through organisations like these.

To the parent of a new starter, the PTA sounds terribly official. The uninitiated may well imagine it being run by a cliquey band of influential, highly organised parents who zealously guard their position as raffle organisers extraordinaire. The truth is often quite the reverse.

In an age when volunteering is about as fashionable as Crimplene, if you show so much as a hint of willingness to help out you'll be stuffing baked beans into jacket potatoes at the next summer fundraiser faster than you can say tombola.

The fact is that parents don't volunteer their time the way they used to. In many families with school-age children, both parents work. What free time they have is always accounted for. Grandparents often live miles away. So who does that leave to stick tombola tickets on 200 prizes or bake a beautifully iced Christmas cake for the annual raffle?

The answer, all too often these days, is hardly anyone. Parents prepared to give up an evening for a committee meeting or palm their children off on to dad at the Christmas fundraiser while they stand for two hours selling pop and crisps are few and far between. If you're willing to help, don't be put off by the fact that you're new to the school. Most PTAs will snap your hand off.

And don't worry that you won't know anyone when you go to that first meeting. The chances are you'll know half the people there. It's always the same people who volunteer for everything. The parents who always washed up at mums and tots, who were first in the queue to donate a raffle prize to playgroup, who are always taking someone else's child home for tea: they're the people you'll see on the PTA.

And thank goodness for them. Rarely are these do-gooders with nothing better to do with their time. They're just people who, despite having as many calls on their time as the next man, are quietly doing their bit to help. The phrase, 'If you want a job doing, ask a busy person,' was made for people like these.

So, why do they bother anyway? The school would hardly grind to a halt if the PTA folded tomorrow. Well, no, but what fundraisers do for schools is pay for the icing on the cake. Schools will never have enough money in their budgets to pay for all the computer equipment they need. They'll never have sufficient money spare for transport to the pantomime, or dressing-up outfits, or sports gear, or a giant snakes and ladders for the playground, or a pottery kiln, or presents for the infants from Father Christmas.

Schools come to rely on fundraising to provide the things that give a school its individuality. The money a good PTA can make gives schools what so many are lacking – a bit of flexibility to do something different. A little spare money goes a long, long way.

If you're interested in finding out more about your school's PTA, ask the school secretary to put you in touch with one of the committee and find out what you could do to help. Remember:

- You're not signing up for life. If you go to one committee meeting and come away feeling it's not for you, you don't have to go again.

- If you don't want the commitment of evening meetings, put your name forward as a willing helper. The committee will be only too pleased to know of a volunteer they can call on to hand out hot dogs at the summer barbecue.
- If nothing else, support their efforts by going along to fundraisers or donating prizes.
- Above all, never criticise the willing. If other parents are prepared to give their time for the good of all the children, don't stand on the sidelines and whinge. Do not be that parent who, tucking into the refreshments laid on after her child's nativity, complained to the PTA that not *all* the mince pies were home-made.

Remember, too, that PTAs shouldn't only be about fundraising. They should also be the catalyst for social events bringing school and families together. And, as the liaison between staff and parents, they provide a chance for requests, grievances and questions to be aired. They might, for instance, organise an evening for parents to be shown around the computer suite and see how their children are being taught information technology.

It's all part of that bigger picture of building a firm partnership between school and home.

There's a great deal of apathy. It's the same parents who turn up every time. But the bottom line is that what you do benefits all the children. Our school wouldn't have a lot of the facilities it has if it wasn't for the PTA.

A committee member

You'll find it's the same right the way through. It's always the same parents who volunteer. The willing parents, the ones who were with you on the playgroup committee, will still be there selling raffle tickets alongside you at a secondary school fundraiser when all your children are sixteen.

The parent of a sixteen-year-old

---

17 BEST FRIENDS?

One of our biggest fears when we send our children to school is that they won't make friends.

We picture our children huddled alone on a bench at playtimes, while all around them the popular children, the ones brought up well by more capable parents, play hopscotch in the sunshine.

Our fears are compounded by the fact that the first time our child is alone for more than five minutes they can't wait for home time to win the sympathy vote from mum with tales of their miserable day. 'I've had a *horrible* time,' they say. '*Nobody* would play with me and I was *all on my own.*'

In reality, few children are left to play on their own day after day. Most find a friend and those who don't are generally helped along the way by a teacher or dinner lady, keen to see that no one gets left out.

But what can you do as a parent if your child is struggling to mix at school? And how can you help your child when those all-important friendships fall apart?

MAKING FRIENDS

In the busy days of early childhood, when life for many children is one long social whirl, many have a ready-made circle of friends from even the youngest age.

Toddler groups, gym tots, swimming sessions and the rest get youngsters used to mixing with other children often before their first birthday. For most of that time, they don't so much play with each other as tolerate each other, and even that sporadically.

They might play alongside each other, but actually playing together is a social skill too far. The most you can reasonably expect is that they don't throw an ear-piercing tantrum when their 'friend' goes within chewing distance of their favourite toy.

As they get older and move on to nursery or pre-school, true friendships start to emerge. Even the closest friends are still more than capable of spectacular fall-outs, but they tend to be quickly forgotten. Their social skills start to develop and they begin to seek out each other's company.

They learn to share, they learn that hitting another child with a fairy wand rarely gets them what they want, and they even start to grasp, thanks to all those endless birthday party invitations, that being out in musical bumps does not signal the end of the world as we know it.

By the time they're ready for school, many will already know lots of the children who are going to be in their class.

Some develop a particularly close bond with another child. They become best friends. They spend lots of time together, share the same interests, make up their own games.

You send them off to school arm in arm, confident that yours won't be the child moping on their own in the corner.

And then, this happens ...

BEST FRIENDS

Those two little girls you sent skipping into school together might well stay joined at the hip. But be prepared. It might not last forever.

They are about to mix with a lot of new children, children who have never appeared before in their social circle. Some of them will be nice, some of them will be exciting, some will appeal as new playmates.

One lunch hour, your child's best friend goes off to play with a new girl. Your child feels hurt, bemused, lonely. It happens again the next day. Your daughter tries to join in, but feels shut out.

Then, horror of horrors, the new girl invites the chosen one home for tea. In your home, there are tears at bedtime.

And the next day, what's the first thing your child sees when she walks into the playground? The new bosom buddies, strolling arm in arm and giggling conspiratorially. If you feel a stab of jealousy – and you will – imagine how your child must be feeling.

Best friendships can fall apart at any time. Sometimes it happens when children first start school and get the chance to make friends of their choosing rather than friends you pretty much chose for them.

Sometimes it happens much later in primary school when children who still spent a lot of time together, both in and out of school hours, suddenly grow apart. Sometimes the split is temporary, sometimes it's permanent. Always, as with all intense relationships, it's painful.

So what should you do to help your child through the crisis? How can you make it all better?

1. Recognise that your child is truly heartbroken. These are genuine feelings. Dismissing them as the emotions of a drama queen won't help anyone.
2. Take them seriously. Treat your child's feelings with respect. Listen to what she has to say.
3. Never ridicule a distressed child. Put yourself in her shoes. Remember that moment when you saw her best friend with someone else. Think about how it made you feel. Don't try to make light of her feelings.
4. Ask gentle questions. Did anything happen that caused the split? Was there a fall-out that could be sorted with a bit of pride swallowing and an apology?
5. Help your child to move on. Explain to her that these things happen in life. Friendships form and friendships break. It's one of the drawbacks of being human. Even adults are upset sometimes when friends lose touch or move away or fall out with them. You can understand why she feels sad, but it will get better. She'll have a chance to make new friends and she can still be friends with her old friend, even if they're not best friends any more.
6. Finally, take heart. However distressed your child is, the chances are she'll get over it much more quickly than an adult would in the same situation.

HOW TO ENCOURAGE NEW FRIENDSHIPS

If you're worried that your child is short of friends, there are steps you can take to help things along.

Children can need a bit of subtle parental help in making new friendships for all sorts of reasons. Maybe you've moved to a new area, maybe an old friendship has broken down, or maybe your child is just not the world's best mixer.

A gentle nudge in the right direction from you might just help to get a new friendship started. Tips you can try include:

- Inviting a child round for tea. Ask your child if there's someone they'd like to have round for a play. Seek guidance from that child's mum so that you're sure of preparing their favourite meal and find out what kind of things they like to do. Then, within reason, try to stand well back and give the two children some space to get on with it. If the visitor has a good time, he'll want to come back and that will mean including your child in his social circle. If it doesn't work out, don't be put off. Try again with a different child.
- Find out from other parents what their children do outside school hours. Swimming lessons, Beavers, judo, dancing classes are all things you could try – though we wouldn't suggest all at once – to encourage your child to mix.
- Ask another mum if her child would like to join you on a social outing. You could offer to take the child with you or invite mum along, too. It could be a bar meal and a romp in a play area, a trip to the cinema, or a girlie tour of the cheap and cheerful accessories shops. And, of course, the best things in life are free. A kick-around in the park with juice and biscuits for half-time will delight most boys – particularly if you can persuade dad to come along in goal and let the visitor score.
- If they play well together, be sure to tell mum in front of her child how well they've behaved. It will boost the child's self-esteem and please mum no end.

If, in spite of all your best efforts, your child is still struggling to mix, have a private word with his teacher and seek her advice. No teacher wants an unhappy child in class. By encouraging your child to work with other children and steering him in the right direction at playtimes, she may well be able to help him beat the playtime blues.

> When best friends fall out, all you can do at the end of the day is mop up the tears and sympathise. You can't force friendships and it's nigh on impossible to interfere. To a large extent, they just have to get on with it.
>
> *The parent of a six-year-old girl*

UNSUITABLE FRIENDSHIPS

Getting in with the wrong crowd can start early. If you're worried that your child has formed a friendship that is leading him down the path to the head's office, you're going to need all the tact you can muster.

Laying down the law is difficult and probably counterproductive, particularly if it means your child announcing in front of his friend's mother the next morning: 'My mum says you're naughty and I'm not allowed to play with you any more.'

Have a serious talk to your child about his behaviour. Tell him that the school won't tolerate him misbehaving and neither will you. Explain that you're disappointed and that you want him to improve. Set up a reward chart if it'll help.

And don't be afraid to consult with the teacher. She'll probably be delighted to do what she can to discourage a terrible twosome.

Again, it may pay you to encourage some new friendships. It's true what they say – that you can't pick your children's friends for them – but, with young children, fish fingers, chips and beans, followed by ice cream with a chocolate flake, can sometimes go a long way to help.

SIBLING RIVALRY

Every child with a brother or sister feels jealous of them sometimes. In every home where there's more than one child, parents will identify with that soulful cry of: 'It's not fair. You love her more than me.'

And this despite the fact that all good parents move heaven and earth to treat their children fairly. They do their best to ensure that their children get equal shares of their attention. They take care not to give more to one than another.

When it comes to sharing out the pocket money, or deciding which child gets to choose their favourite TV programme, or ruling whose turn it is for the cheesiest slice of pizza, it's easy to ensure equal shares with the treats.

But what if one child is born with above-average intelligence and the other is an academic struggler? How do you make that fair?

GREAT EXPECTATIONS

When we decide to have a second child, most of us expect it to be something like the first. The new baby might look different, he might have a quite different personality, but all too often we assume that intellectually the two won't be poles apart.

Three years on, when child number two is showing not the slightest interest in learning the letters child number one had mastered before playgroup, alarm bells start to ring. What if this child is going to struggle with the things his brother found easy? What if he's languishing in the bottom set while his brother cruises along in the top group? How unfair is that?

Of course, the difference between the brothers, the thing that makes life a bed of roses for one and a clamber through nettles for the other, may have nothing to do with intellect. One might have superb concentration while the other is never still for two minutes together. One might be a gifted footballer and the other have all the co-ordination of a jelly. One might have enough friends to start a youth club and the other could be a bit of a loner.

What as a parent can you do to stop one growing up smug and the other nursing a lifelong chip on their shoulder?

BROTHERLY LOVE

So crushed can one child feel by his parents' apparent favouritism of a sibling, that Americans, not surprisingly, have invented a name for it. They call it Sibling Rivalry Disorder – presumably SRD for short.

A child brought up in a family where he is constantly compared unfavourably with his supposedly far-superior sibling is hardly likely to grow up brimming with self-esteem. When he goes to school and finds his nose rubbed in his own shortcomings in areas where his brother excelled, the feelings of inadequacy can be overwhelming.

Some shrink into the isolated life of a loner. Others become that annoying, hyped-up, supremely silly child you dread having round to play because you know that within five minutes of arriving he'll be swinging from the lampshade and feeding popping candy to the dog.

What *is* he doing? Getting attention any way he can, that's what. Even attention from a fuming adult and a terrified dog that thinks Bonfire Night has come early is better than no attention at all.

You want to treat your children as equals, but how do you do that when one child has apparently been dealt a poorer hand than another?

1. Be on your guard. Catch yourself making more of one child than another. Those cries of, 'It's not fair!' may ring out in every household, but sometimes they're right – it's not. If the claim is justified, talk over your child's grievance and see if you can make it fairer. Do you spend longer helping your gifted child with homework

because you know he can excel? Do you spend less with the child who's struggling? Don't write him off. He needs your help just as much. He probably needs it more. By the same token, be on your guard against trying to even up the score by giving an unfair share of your attention to the less able child. Beware of building resentment by lavishing praise on the less gifted child and not giving equal praise to the achievements of his brother.

2. Don't compare your children. You might wish the younger could make friends like the elder, but never be tempted to say so. Don't even say it to another adult when you think they're not listening. Children's confidence has been destroyed by far less.

3. Don't tolerate teachers comparing your children with each other. Teachers are not perfect, they don't always think before they speak. Children still sometimes get that stinging: 'You're a different kettle of fish to your brother. I had no problems when he was in my class. It was a real pleasure to teach him.' However confident the child might seem, that hurts. Have a quiet word with the teacher if necessary. Explain that your children might be different, but that you're working hard to give both the confidence to succeed.

4. Never forget that each child is his own person. Celebrate the triumphs and strengths of both children. Make the most of their talents and abilities. A weaker child who feels loved and valued may never get that first from Oxford like his brother, but should still have the confidence in his own achievements.

And don't fear too much for the less-gifted child. Bear in mind that in all families, even the ones where the talent is equally shared, jealousy still rears its ugly head. All siblings argue sometimes. All have feelings of resentment over something a brother or sister has achieved. Getting to grips with their feelings might not be easy, but it's great practice for life in the world outside.

A NEW BABY

There's nothing quite like a new baby to shake up the universe of a young child.

For a school-age child, the arrival of a new baby can be a lot to take in. If it coincides with him starting school, it can be doubly difficult.

Seen through your child's eyes, he's just been sent off to school while the new baby gets mum to himself. Why has she had this baby anyway? Is it because she was tired of the child she'd already got?

Tempting as it is to expect a school-age child to take the whole thing in his stride, remember that he's going to need lots of reassurance.

Do everything you can to show him that his place in the family is secure. Find time for him when he comes in from school. Tell him that, however much you love the new baby, you miss having your big boy to talk to. Try to get an hour off at the weekend that's just for the two of you. Make him feel just as special as he always has and, rest assured, you'll get there in the end.

WORRIERS

All children worry at some time, but some seem destined to make it their life's work.

These are the children who worry about anything and everything. They would rather put their favourite toy through a shredder than fail to hand their homework in on time. They dread the annual school play for fear that they'll fluff their two lines. They get five out of six in the weekly spelling test and spend the rest of the day worrying about the one they got wrong.

And they live in permanent fear of being in trouble. Such is their obsession with rules that they would rather walk barefoot over burning coals than take the shortcut home via the field and risk being caught scaling the fence at the other end.

It's quite normal for children to worry sometimes. Some worries, like a fear of being separated from mum, or a fear of strangers are not just normal, they're perfectly sensible and useful emotions to have. But for some children, worrying is so ingrained that there's a real danger of it spoiling what should be the carefree days of childhood.

Often, the worry turns into shyness. Then the parent starts to worry and they start to tell people that their child is shy, and that worries the child even more – and on, and on it goes.

Almost always, when children are worrying excessively there's a reason for it. Of course, there are a lot of reasons why it might be happening. It *might* be bullying, but it's probably far more likely that the reason is uncomfortably closer to home. In all too many cases, where a child is worrying too much, it's because unrealistic expectations are being demanded of him. He might be fretting over only getting five out of six spellings right, but is that because he knows dad would have wanted him to get the full house?

If your child is a worrier:

1. Be there to talk over his concerns and offer reassurance.
2. Give honest explanations. So if, for instance, your child is worrying that something terrible is going to happen, sit down and talk through his concerns. Don't fob him off with a dismissive: 'That's just a silly worry.' Give him a truthful, factual answer.
3. Ask yourself whether you're asking too much of him.
4. Make a conscious effort to give your child attention when he's *not* worried. In some families, children learn that it's only when you're worried that you get mum's undivided attention.
5. Keep stressing the things he is good at. Put the emphasis on the things he does well and build his confidence.

If you're still concerned that worrying is spoiling school for your child, talk to the teacher. If she shares your concerns, she'll want to do whatever she can to build up his self-esteem.

One tried and tested trick is to pair up a young worrier to work with the most laid-back, worry-free child in the class. With a bit of luck, some of the cool customer's attitude will rub off on the worrier. And if the teacher is really lucky, some of the fretful child's conscientiousness might just rub off on Mr Cool.

> I was a terrible worrier at school. It definitely spoiled my schooldays. My greatest hope was that I wouldn't pass that on to my child. He's not as bad as I was, but the thought of being in trouble still terrifies him.
>
> *The mother of a seven-year-old*

18 SPECIAL EDUCATIONAL NEEDS

'Special educational needs' is one of those phrases which is widely used and hugely misunderstood.

There are parents who think their child has special educational needs (SEN) when clearly they do not. And there are parents who deny that their child has special needs when clearly they do.

And in the melee between them come the parents of children who fall into neither camp and have virtually no idea what the phrase actually means in practice. Some think all special needs children should go to special schools. Others think any seven-year-old unable to spell 'accommodation' warrants the title.

Why the confusion? Because not so long ago children considered to have a disability were generally spirited away from mainstream education. Children with physical or mental disabilities were often educated in special schools with others who had similar problems.

Now, the emphasis is on picking up children with special educational needs as early in their lives as possible and giving them that crucial early help that could make all the difference to their development.

So, what are special educational needs, and how do you know if your child needs extra help?

WHAT ARE SPECIAL EDUCATIONAL NEEDS?

The first thing to clear up is that SEN is not a term applied willy-nilly to children who fail to make good progress in school.

All children learn at different speeds and in different ways. If your child is twelve reading books behind the high-fliers and sometimes needs extra help, don't assume that he has special needs.

Teachers are trained to choose the most appropriate way of teaching each individual child. If a pupil seems to be having particular difficulties in one area, they might well be given extra help or different lessons to help them along. They may be given special 'catch-up' work to get them up to speed. It doesn't necessarily mean they have special educational needs.

The legal definition is that all children with special educational needs have learning difficulties or disabilities which make it harder for them to learn than most children of the same age. Children with SEN may need extra help because of a range of problems, such as in thinking or understanding, physical or sensory difficulties, emotional or behavioural problems, or how they relate to and behave with other people.

They may have difficulties with speech and language, though the law specifically states that children do not have learning difficulties just because their first language is not English.

It is far from unusual for a child to have special educational needs at some stage in their schooling. With the right support, many children' overcome their problems quickly and easily, but there are some who will need extra support long term – and for some that will mean throughout their time in school.

Special educational needs is a term covering a huge range of problems. Children could have difficulties with, for instance:

- All of the work in school
- Reading, writing, maths or understanding information
- Expressing themselves or understanding what others are saying
- Making friends or relating to adults
- Behaving
- Organising themselves
- Physical or sensory difficulties

WHAT HAPPENS TO CHILDREN WITH SPECIAL EDUCATIONAL NEEDS?

It is now usual for children with special educational needs to be given the help they need in the child's ordinary, mainstream pre-school or school, sometimes with support from outside specialists. There are, of course, still special schools that provide a setting particularly suited to some children.

WHAT SHOULD YOU DO IF YOU ARE WORRIED ABOUT YOUR CHILD?

The first and crucial thing is not to worry alone. No one knows your child as well as you, and if you think there may be a problem, it's best to talk to a professional about your concerns.

The earlier special educational needs are identified, the better. Some are picked up in routine development screening by doctors and health visitors. But if you have worries of your own, don't wait until a routine appointment comes round. Go and seek help straight away. Health professionals will be able to advise you of the next step, if any, that you should take.

If your child is at school or a pre-school and you feel they may have a special educational need that has not been picked up, talk to one of the staff about your concerns. Arrange to see the child's teacher, the head teacher, or the SENCO (the person in a school or pre-school who has a particular responsibility for co-ordinating help for children with special educational needs).

Explain what your worries are and ask for their opinion. It may well be that what seems to you to be a huge problem is nothing of the sort. The teacher may well be able to reassure you that the difficulties your child is experiencing are perfectly normal. By working with the teacher, it could be that the extra support you give your child will be enough to spur on his development.

WHAT HAPPENS IF YOUR FEARS ARE WELL FOUNDED?

Of course, some parents' fears are all too real. What may come as some reassurance is that mainstream schools are geared up like never before to give appropriate support to children with SEN. And they also have an obligation to put you, as parents, at the centre of decisions affecting your child.

The basic principles that guide schools in England are:

- All children with special educational needs should have their needs met
- Those needs are normally met in mainstream schools and pre-schools
- Your views as parents, and the wishes of your child, should be listened to
- You, as parents, have a vital role in supporting your child's education
- Children with special educational needs should be given a broad, well-balanced and relevant education

As soon as a problem is picked up, your child's school or pre-school will start to introduce changes to help him. But there is no obvious one-size-fits-all measure they can take to improve his learning.

All children are different, whether they have special needs or not. Children can have different kinds of special educational needs and the severity of the difficulty can vary enormously. Like all children, they learn in different ways.

Because there is no definitive answer to each problem, the best way forward is known in the jargon as the 'graduated approach'. What it means is that, increasingly, a school can bring in the specialist expertise it needs step-by-step to help a particular child. By working methodically, the school and specialists should be able to build up a package of extra help that best suits that child and his own unique situation.

None of this will happen behind your back. The school must tell you when it first starts giving extra or different help for your child because of their special educational needs. It might be something as simple as introducing a different way of teaching in some areas that might best suit your child. It might be help from another member of staff, perhaps working with children in small groups. Or it could mean introducing a physical change, such as bringing in a computer for him to work on.

Your child might need that extra help for just a short time. But it's possible that, despite all the school's best efforts, he still doesn't make enough progress. At that stage, specialist help may be brought in from outside: for example, from a speech and language therapist or an educational psychologist.

In some, relatively few, cases the Local Education Authority may decide to carry out a more detailed assessment of your child's needs. The authority might then write a statement of special educational needs, which basically describes the child's problems and all the special help they need.

You, as parents, or the school or pre-school, can request a statutory assessment, and the Local Education Authority will then decide whether it is justified. The authority will usually make a statement if it decides that all the special help your child needs cannot be provided from within the school's resources.

If an assessment goes ahead, you will still have a right to say which state school you want your child to go to, whether mainstream or special. It can be the school he already attends. The Local Education Authority must go along with your preference as long as the school is suitable for your child's age, ability and needs, that admitting your child to the school won't harm the education of other pupils, and that it is an efficient use of the authority's resources.

Special schools usually take children with particular special needs, but many ordinary schools also provide particular special help. Some mainstream schools offer special teaching for children with hearing difficulties, for instance, or dyslexia.

Remember that your views count. You should be at the heart of the decision-making all the way through. Professionals no longer just pay lip service to what parents think, because it's now widely recognised that parents really do know their child best and their opinion is worth listening to.

You can ask for extra help, you can put your views, and you can appeal against some decisions. And you can take advice from the many organisations that might be able to help you and your child.

Parent partnership services are there to provide accurate and neutral information on the full range of options open to parents whose children have special needs. Your Local Education Authority will have their details.

And there are also many national and local voluntary organisations, mainly charities, which may be able to help.

YOUR CHILD, YOUR CHOICE

There has been a sea change in attitudes to children with special needs. The buzz word in schools now is 'inclusion' – giving all children the chance of a broad education, no matter what difficulties may stand in the way.

The move to give more children with SEN a chance to go to a mainstream school has brought immense advantages. Children with special needs are accepted as part of the community with the same rights as everyone else to achieve their potential.

And the gain has not been all one-sided. Other children have gained, too, by accepting their classmates with special needs and learning some eye-opening lessons in life from them.

So, is everything in the garden lovely? Of course not. You can't expect a child with behavioural problems to slot into a mainstream school without ever causing problems. You can't conjure up a best friend for a lonely child whose special needs set him apart in the playground.

And you can't make your child what he isn't. One of the dilemmas for parents of children with special educational needs is that they must sometimes seem overwhelmed by the extra work they are expected to do with their child at the end of a long school day.

As a parent, you will obviously want to do your best for your child. You will move mountains to make sure your child gets the extra help he needs, both at school and at home. The temptation to push and go on pushing must be immense. But never lose sight of the fact that this is still a child, your child, with the same rights to a good education as all the rest – but the same rights to a childhood, too.

DYSLEXIA

Many children take to reading and writing with effortless skill. Many don't.

Lots of children find it very difficult to learn to read and write. It is, after all, a complex skill that we're asking our children to master, often a full year before most of us had even started school.

But for the parents of those who are struggling, it can be a terrible time. Who wouldn't feel the panic rising when their child stayed resolutely on the most basic of picture books while many of their classmates were romping ahead?

Before long, alarm bells start to ring. Is there something seriously wrong with my child? Could he be dyslexic?

The answer is, almost certainly not. Children are not machines, pre-programmed to start reading on their fourth birthday. Early difficulties are not uncommon and many of those who seem slow off the mark soon catch up with a bit of extra help.

But sometimes, just sometimes, there is an underlying problem holding children back. And sometimes it *is* dyslexia.

If you're worried, there are signs you can look out for that might help you to decide whether you should consider further testing. Your child may not show all of them, but a significant number might warrant seeking advice from the professionals.

- **Writing:** Children with dyslexia often have problems learning and remembering spelling. Many have poor writing compared with how they can express themselves verbally.
- **Reading:** Dyslexic children have difficulty in identifying separate sounds in words. They find it hard to read simple common words, and have problems with unusual pronunciation.

- **Ordering:** Many struggle to organise and complete simple tasks; they have problems understanding time concepts – yesterday, today, tomorrow. They might find it hard to remember sequential orders, such as months of the year, or a list of instructions.
- **Lack of concentration:** Some are easily distracted. It can be tough for them to follow simple directions like left and right. And relatively simple tasks so sap their concentration that they might easily feel very tired.

If several of these warning signs ring true, you may want to talk over your concerns with your child's teacher or the school's SEN co-ordinator.

Try not to worry. If it is dyslexia, lots can be done to help and the sooner the problem is identified, the better. Given the help they need, many dyslexic children go on to do very well.

GIFTED CHILDREN

Children who are exceptionally talented also have special needs that need to be addressed by schools. Just as those with learning difficulties need extra attention, so children who are outstandingly gifted need to have their talents nurtured.

The onus on teachers is to make learning both challenging and enjoyable, whatever a child's ability. All pupils, including the gifted and talented, should be given the chance to achieve their full potential.

By earmarking pupils as exceptionally skilled in particular areas, teachers try to ensure that the children are stretched and encouraged throughout their schooling. For some pupils, it may mean a chance to study some or all subjects at a greater depth and breadth.

In primary schools, there is an added complication. As well as stretching a child's intellect, teachers have to bear in mind that, however talented, these are still young children. The teachers' task is to encourage them in developing their natural skills without in any way neglecting their need to grow and mature just like all the other children. Social skills and emotional development are just as vital to *every* child.

19 A PARENT'S ROLE

We have looked a lot at what you should expect from your child's school. But what should the school be able to expect from you?

HOME–SCHOOL AGREEMENTS

Sounds very formal, doesn't it, a home–school agreement? And in many ways, it is.

All state schools in England have them and all parents are asked to sign them. What they amount to is a formal agreement: you promise to support the school's policies, and they promise to support you and your child.

Each school will have its own agreement, drawn up initially in consultation with parents. They look a bit like a cross between a company's mission statement and a simple contract of employment.

Areas they are likely to cover include:

- **Standards:** A pledge about the standard of education the school aims to provide. There might, for instance, be a reference to the children's right to a broad curriculum, and how the school aims to meet the needs of all children.
- **The ethos of the school:** Just what is it that sets it apart from others? There may be a reference to how the ethos of the school is reflected in the attitudes of staff, and the way pupils relate to staff and to each other. It may set out the school's aims for being part of the community, and it may refer to how it intends to nurture the pupils' spiritual, moral, cultural and social development.
- **Attendance:** There is likely to be a reminder of the need to send your child to school not just regularly, but on time. Few bad habits irk a teacher more than the pupil who strolls in ten minutes late every morning looking like any time before lunch will do. Remember, too, that you don't have a *right* to take children on

holiday in term-time. The school must agree this beforehand and the indications are that schools are likely to be encouraged to get tougher on term-time absences in the future.

- **Discipline and behaviour:** Nothing is more harmful to a school's stance on discipline than the parent who consistently undermines the authority of the teaching staff. Good behaviour and discipline have to spring from a partnership between home and school. The home–school agreement will almost certainly spell out the need for the pupil to abide by the school's rules. You will be asked to play your part by supporting the school in maintaining good discipline.
- **Homework:** The government recommends that all children from Year One upwards should be given regular homework. The agreement should ask you to support the school's homework policy. If the policy is not spelled out in detail, you can ask to see it in full.
- **Communication:** The agreement may include a pledge from the school on the part it will play in communicating with you on issues affecting the school and your child. It may also ask for your co-operation in keeping the school informed of any issues that may affect your child's work or behaviour.

After you have had a chance to read the agreement, the school will ask you to sign it and return it to school. If you subsequently break the agreement, you may be asked to discuss the issue with the head teacher, but this is only likely to happen in practice if there is a serious problem with discipline. And even then it's hardly likely that the main thrust of the interview will revolve around why you broke the agreement when the more pressing issue is that your child has just floored a classmate.

So, do the agreements really matter at all? Well, there's certainly an argument for saying no. Like many a company's mission statement before them, hours are lavished on drawing them up but six months down the line no one can actually remember what they say.

But home–school agreements do have one advantage that company policies generally lack. What they spell out to parents from the very beginning is that the school values their input.

By getting parents to put their signature on an official document, what the school is saying is that this is a partnership. However the issues are phrased, the message the school is getting across is that we as teachers, and you as parents, both have a responsibility to your child. By working together, we can not only help your child to learn, but to mature and grow into a responsible young person.

It's not only asking for help, it's getting down there in black and white that the input of parents is needed, valued, welcomed and crucial. And if that's the message parents take away, it's surely worth the effort.

PARENTS' EVENINGS

Parents' evenings are, without doubt, one of the most unnerving experiences you'll undergo as the parent of a schoolchild.

However talkative your child, and however involved you are as a parent, it's very hard to be sure how he gets on at school.

Has the child who would rather die than sing for his granny got the confidence to put his hand up and ask questions in class? How does this child, still well capable of throwing a foot-stomping paddy if he loses at Top Trumps, behave when you're not around? And, if he's so reluctant to do homework for you, is he any better for the teacher?

At parents' evening, for good or bad, all is revealed. And in perhaps far more detail than you might have imagined.

A school will invite you to attend a parents' evening at least once a year. Many slot in at least one more – and so they should. If schools are serious about education being a partnership between teacher and parent, they can hardly justify holding a formal meeting with parents just once a year.

Don't be surprised if you're called to your first parents' evening very soon after your child starts school or moves to a new class. This is an opportunity for you to meet the teacher and for the teacher to meet you. They'll tell you how your child is settling in and a good teacher will also want to know from you how things are at home. If your child is losing sleep over school or is refusing point blank to have anything to do with homework, the teacher will want to know.

Even this early in the year, the teacher will already have made some assessments about your child's strengths and weaknesses. You may be surprised by what you hear. A child, particularly a less confident child, who comes home with tales of how badly he's doing in maths may actually be doing quite well. By the same token, an over-confident child may not be doing as well as he thinks.

Most teachers will pull no punches. They'll give you a fair and honest assessment of how your child is getting on. But they will try to be as positive as they can and you should do the same.

Don't do that terrible thing that adults do when someone is trying to give an honest assessment of your performance. You know, that bit in your work appraisal where after twenty minutes of glowing compliments, your boss says something like: 'Your work is always good and very thorough, but perhaps you could make it one of your aims to speed up just a little.' And all you take away from the whole experience is that he thinks you're slow.

Don't do that to your child. If the teacher says your child is working well, that his work is of an acceptable standard, and that his behaviour is good, don't go away worrying about the bit where she said he could be a post-lunch daydreamer.

The crucial question, whatever the standard of his work, should be: is he trying his best? And if he is, go home satisfied and give him a hug because you can't ask any more than that.

HOW TO MAKE THE MOST OF PARENTS' EVENINGS

This is a rare opportunity to hear the full lowdown on how your child is doing. So you want to make the most of it:

1. Give it top priority. Both parents should go if possible, not least so that both of you hear exactly what the teacher has to say rather than one of you just hearing the edited highlights. If it really is impossible for you to make it on the day, have a word with the teacher – they may be prepared to see you at a different time.
2. Do your homework. Think about the things you want to find out and, if you think it'll help, write yourself a crib list so that you don't get waylaid. Time is short and precious. If you're not careful, you'll be out ten minutes later having been spoken at by a teacher who hasn't addressed the questions you've been burning to ask.
3. Expect very specific information about your child's progress. The teacher will tell you how your child is faring in different subject areas, and should paint you a clear picture of what your child is like in class.
4. Listen to what the teacher is saying – even if it's not what you want to hear. If the teacher has grounds for criticism or needs to point out weaknesses, she's doing it for the good of your child. Instead of going on the defensive, ask what she suggests to improve things and see if you can work together to help your child succeed. And fix a follow-up meeting to check on progress.
5. Don't over-run your time if there's a queue of other parents behind you. If you feel there wasn't time to cover everything you wanted to talk about, ask if you can see the teacher by appointment on a different day.

Parents' evenings are important, but in most schools they only come around very infrequently. If you have a problem – if your child seems to be struggling, if they're unhappy in school, if they're misbehaving – don't wait until the next parents' evening to sort it out. A good teacher will always make time to see you if you have concerns.

> After a parents' evening, you should ask yourself, 'Does the person I've been talking to know my child? Do they know his work?' What matters to the individual parent is the individual. They want to know how the school responds to *their* child. And they want to know that, if their child was unhappy, the school would care.
>
> *A head teacher*

SCHOOL REPORTS

The end of the school year. The sealed brown envelope with your parents' names on the front. The deathly hush while your parents sat reading through the contents. The anxious wait to find out what it said.

Ring any bells? If you thought it was nerve-racking taking your own school report home, wait until your child brings his home for you to read.

Today's school reports, even for infants, are a very formal affair. Not for schools these days some bland statement about your child's progress and behaviour. Expect a report that is long, detailed and (sometimes painfully) honest.

What the teacher writes will generally sum up their observations of your child based on how well he has performed in tests and assignments, to what extent he participates in class discussion and activities, and how he behaves.

And you can expect their achievements and shortcomings to be listed subject by subject, from the obvious literacy and numeracy down to PE.

Most schools produce their formal report at the end of the school year, but not all schools do detailed reports for reception children because of the wealth of information they receive through the new and very detailed report, the Foundation Stage Profile.

WHAT WILL YOU LEARN FROM YOUR CHILD'S REPORT?

Probably more than you were expecting. A typical report, even for an infant, might have ten or more national curriculum subjects listed with a report on the progress made in each. You'd expect to hear how your six-year-old is doing in English, but a report on his progress in information and communication technology might come as a surprise.

A good report is far more than simply a record of a child's achievements. It should be a window into that closed world of the classroom. The teacher's remarks should give you an idea of how confident your child is, how enthusiastic, how much he enjoys the work. It can be an eye-opener to a parent who faces the daily 'Do we *have* to go to school?' debate over the Frosties.

And while the teacher will do her best to accentuate the positive, a good report will also list your child's shortcomings. If your child is prone to fidgeting, or has the pencil control of Mr Jelly, or is always last to finish, expect to see it in the report. The whole exercise would be pretty pointless otherwise.

Your child's teacher might also set him aims for the year ahead, whether blatantly listed as 'targets' or more subtly implied. Take the hint – this has been written for you. If the teacher writes: 'He must continue to learn number bonds,' he's hardly likely to think 'Whoopee!' and apply himself throughout the summer holidays. It's down to you to drop in the occasional maths teaser to help him brush up his skills.

As with all formal reports, you may have to read between the lines. When a teacher writes a PE report that states: 'Demonstrates some level of skill in a range of activities', realise that what she possibly held back was, 'but, frankly, not much'.

Be aware, too, that many teachers write their reports using computer programs containing banks of statements from which they can draw. A teacher might, for instance, click on to a statement saying, 'Making excellent progress in maths' and the phrase would be transferred into a child's report. It's a sensible, time-saving measure. Where it can go wrong is if teachers pull in phrases that include too much jargon and are therefore unintelligible to parents. If there is anything in your child's report that you don't understand, have no hesitation in asking the teacher exactly what it means. It's possible they don't know either!

Finally, when you've read and re-read the report, and shown it to your partner, and read it again, go back and read it together one more time. Forget all those nagging phrases that you can't get out of your head, the ones about needing to concentrate more and forgetting instructions, and count how many times the teacher says something positive about your child. The chances are that the positives will far outweigh the negatives.

And don't forget the little person who's done all the work. Read the report to him; let him hear what his teacher had to say, good and bad. Then remind him of all the good things she said and do your best – as his teacher almost certainly has – to end the year on a positive note. Come September, he's got to find the confidence to impress a new teacher and do it all over again.

> Most teachers will try to home in on the positive, but if you don't include a child's shortcomings, you're not being truthful. What you're doing is leading the parents up the garden path.
> *An infant-school teacher*
>
> I was amazed at the amount of detail in my five-year-old's school report. I'm a secondary school teacher and I've been through the same amount of training as the primary school teachers, but the more I see the more I realise that I couldn't do their job in a million years. How they cope with that many children, all so different, and know them so well, I just don't know. It is such an important job.
> *A mother and teacher*

PUSHY PARENTS

We have all come across pushy parents. They stand out from the crowd not so much because they want their children to do well, but because they are prepared to pay almost any price to achieve it.

If their child rushes out of school flushed with the news that he just got 29 out of 30 in a maths test, their first question will always be: 'Which one did you get wrong?'

They brag incessantly about their child's achievements and push him relentlessly to ensure there's always something fresh to brag about.

They do Kumon maths after school on Mondays 'because he can't get enough of numbers', chess club on Tuesdays where 'he likes to play with adults, they're more on his wavelength', computer club on Wednesdays because 'he wants to learn how to improve the school website', and orchestra on Thursdays ('his teacher says he's such a gifted musician'). On Fridays mum and child relax at home with a few SATs revision books because 'he's so determined to do well'.

For which read, his parents are so determined he should do well.

Despite the fact that he's clearly excelling at school, his parents are not averse to bad-mouthing the teachers. 'We don't think they're pushing him hard enough. It's all very well having the special needs children in the same class, but they're the ones who get all the attention. The gifted children like ours race through the work and are left twiddling their thumbs. Frankly, he's bored. He'd be better at home.'

What his parents conveniently forget is that their child is sacrificing his childhood to their ambition.

Thankfully, though competition in schools has never been hotter, the over-the-top pushy parent remains a relative rarity. Some still do request an audience with the head to demand more homework or a 'better' reading book for their child, and some still do overlook the fact that, however gifted he may be, he needs to play, he needs to have friends and he needs to unwind.

Unrealistic expectations can ruin what should be a happy family time. The child may do well, he may do very well, but for all his mother's boasting, he'll grow up knowing that his best was rarely good enough. And, however successful he becomes, his achievements will always be overshadowed by the fact that he never had time to be a child.

So take heart the next time a pushy parent is bending your ear about their son's latest achievements and commiserating over your child's shortcomings. No amount of success is worth the loss of a childhood.

20 THE OPTIONAL EXTRAS AND THE SOCIAL SIDE OF SCHOOL

With the national curriculum meaning that most of what happens in school comes as standard, it's the optional extras that help to set schools apart from each other.

SPORT AND THE ARTS

The extra activities laid on by schools hardly register with many parents at the time they're making those crucial decisions about which school to choose. It is hard, after all, ever to imagine your four-year-old growing into one of those strapping lads who stay behind for cricket practice at the end of school.

But the sport and other out-of-school activities could come to be a big part of your child's school life. And you've no idea how appreciative you might be one day of a school that organises the after-school netball practice that entices your nine-year-old away from another night in front of the telly.

Every school, of course, offers different options and it's worth finding out right from the start what's on offer at the schools you're considering for your child. You might find it's an eye-opener in more ways than one. A school which offers lots of activities at the end of the day is likely to be blessed with a particularly conscientious staff, prepared to put in that extra effort for the children.

And a school that, for instance, offers a fair range of sport is showing encouraging signs of not putting all its eggs in the academic league table basket.

If you can envisage your child taking part in sport as he grows older, ask about:

- The range of sports on offer.
- Whether the school encourages everyone who wants to be involved to take part. Can, for instance, girls play in the school football

team? Would a child with the athletic ability of a tapeworm still be made welcome if they wanted to have a bash at cricket?

- Do they take part in inter-schools tournaments? Do they ever win?
- How do they encourage children with real sporting talent?
- What's on offer in PE lessons for the juniors?
- What facilities are there? Remember, not all schools have their own sports field.
- Do they have a sports day and what form does it take?
- What about learning to swim? Relatively few primary schools have their own pool, but a lot take children along to the local town pool for swimming lessons.
- Is there a charge for after-school sports? Some schools offer courses run by commercial organisations that charge for lessons.

Of course, those added extras should be far more than just sport. Music is another big attraction for many children and those first squeaky notes on the dreaded recorder have led to a lifelong interest in music for many.

It's worth finding out what provision the school makes to encourage children to enjoy music. Many schools have a choir and orchestra, and most offer some form of music lessons, sometimes provided by a staff teacher, sometimes run by a musician who tours lots of schools. Again, you may want to find out about the cost and frequency of music lessons.

And do ask about drama. Drama has graduated from an annual appearance in the school nativity to becoming a big part of many children's schooling, particularly as they get older. Drama courses are now hugely popular in many secondary schools and a great way of building self-esteem in younger children. Ask about school productions and theatre visits.

There may, of course, be lots of other activities offered at your child's school. Schools which offer the most over and above the required minimum are more likely to be doing their best to encourage achievement in *all* their pupils, not just the academic high-fliers.

As with everything, your input is vital. Offer your help if you can. The school football team might well be glad of someone to offer help with transport – or, oh joy, to wash those muddy football shirts. But, if that amazingly doesn't appeal, there's one obvious way you can lend your support to your budding David Beckham. Dig out your thermals. As a keen supporter, you're going to need them.

AFTER-SCHOOL CLUBS AND CHILDCARE

If you're a working parent and thought childcare was a nightmare *before* your child started school, you might be in for a nasty shock once your child is there.

At least childcare for pre-school children is designed to fit in with parents' working hours. School hours for many parents who work must seem designed to be as awkward as possible.

For a start, school generally begins at about the same time as most parents are supposed to be at their desks. The result is that many drop their children at the school gates, often parking dangerously on yellow zigzags to do so, and then zoom off to work, arriving just in time to see the boss taking a pointed glance at the office clock.

Either that or they drop their children in the playground half an hour or more before the bell goes and hope that they'll survive until 9 a.m. with virtually no adult supervision. You can imagine how well that goes down with the teachers.

For part-time workers lucky enough to have secured a job with supposedly child-friendly hours, the end of the day is no less stressful. As the clock clicks round to three, they have to be out of the office like a champion greyhound to have any hope of being at school for the 3.30 p.m. bell.

They drive at breakneck speed into the chaos that surrounds virtually all primary schools at home time. They arrive to find that all the best parking spaces have already been taken by parents who turned up at three o'clock rather than face the inconvenience of walking 200 yards.

So the last-gasp Larrys have to park three streets away and run at full pelt, arriving just in time to see their forlorn child returning uncollected to the classroom where the teacher gives mum that same disapproving stare they get from colleagues as they dash from the office the minute their hours are up.

For full-timers, the problems are no less acute – and, for many, far greater than they ever were before their child started school. Nurseries are geared up for parents who need to drop their children off at 8.30 a.m. and collect them at 5.30 p.m. Most schools are not.

That leaves conscientious parents with a big problem. Most are left hunting for those scarce childminders who earn their living on the school run. They will take your child to school in the mornings and collect them at the end of the day. They'll look after them until your work is finished, and some will even give them a meal. Then they'll step in during the school holidays and cover for all those days when you're at work and the children are off. The good ones will give them stimulating things to do rather than fill the gap with two hours of nonstop TV. The downside is that they are, not surprisingly, as easy to find as snow in August.

Even if you've had a childminder for years, don't assume that she'll be able to help out once your child is at school. Many will want to move on and take in younger children needing all-day care.

Another option is schools that run breakfast or after-school clubs. Lots of schools have now gone down this route, recognising the problems parents face, but many have not.

If it's something you're considering, do look into it carefully. For a young child – and for many older ones, too, come to that – a school day stretching from 9 a.m. to 3.30 p.m. can seem endless. Adding on an hour at the beginning and maybe another couple of hours at the end must seem an eternity.

To complicate matters still further, there are all those long school holidays to think about. Even if you and your partner have five weeks each and take them separately, there are still acres of holiday time to cover. Without nursery or a childminder to fall back on, you could really come unstuck unless you plan ahead.

If you've no saintly grandparents prepared to fill the gaps, your best bet is probably to ask around among other parents in the same boat. Holiday clubs might well be the answer, but make sure you know what you're letting your child in for. Do they offer activities that would appeal to your child? Are they appropriate for his age group? Do they ever leave the premises?

Think back to when you were at school. Remember how precious school holidays were. Even if you can't spend all of them with your child, you owe it to them to find some way of making the holidays special rather than just an inconvenience between one term and the next.

You'll also need contingency plans for the teacher-training days when schools close for an odd day (often tagged on to a holiday). And you'll need to think about what will happen that first school morning when your child gets up the colour of cold porridge and vomits into his Rice Krispies. What, even more confusingly, will you do the first time he says, 'I don't feel very well,' but looks like an advert for Sanatogen?

Talk to your employer, talk to your friends, talk to your child-carers. Be prepared for what you're going to do.

So, yes, school will take some of your childcare headaches away. It may throw up more than it solves. But do try, in the midst of it all, to remember the child in all this. From the moment he starts at school, you're not the only one facing a hard day at the office. He's got a long, hard day ahead of him, too.

CHRISTMAS

It's known in some educational circles as 'the C word'.

Christmas may come only once a year, but if you're a teacher it seems to last two months. From the moment the new commercial horror of Halloween is over, children start to go Christmas crazy. They buzz around the teacher like a fly at a light bulb, hyped up to the nines by a hard sell that's all around them – in the shops, on the television, in the home.

To their eternal credit, many teachers love Christmas and still manage to enjoy it as a special time – despite having to walk the fine tightrope between the innocent and the worldly wise. Even in the infants, there's always some little devil desperate to spoil the magic by insisting that there's no Father Christmas and that he's getting his new bike in the Halfords sale.

As for getting children interested in the true meaning of Christmas, teachers must feel like they're wading through quicksand. Ask any youngsters what the best thing is about Christmas, and hand an instant sainthood to any child who doesn't say 'presents'.

The school nativity production is a minefield for schools everywhere. Again, it's true that most children are satisfied with their lot – though expect the odd tantrum when a girl with her heart set on being the Angel Gabriel finds she's an ox instead.

But generally it's the parents who get twitchy. 'How come *she's* been chosen to be Mary again? She's already had her turn at playgroup.'

Schools just can't win. If they go for a Christmas play instead of the traditional nativity, there's hell to pay when they hand out the speaking parts. 'Why has he got eight lines and mine only got two? Why has she been chosen for the fairy dance when she doesn't even go to dancing class?'

And, as for the big production day, well, if you're a school nativity virgin, you're in for a big shock. For a start, you'll find that some parents arrive so early to commandeer the best seats that it's only a matter of time before someone camps overnight.

Teachers will identify with the familiar tale of one mother who, on the day of the school play, stood at the hall door while the lunchtime tables were being cleared away, ran to the first seat put out on the front row, and sat there, arms folded across ample bosom, while the staff put out the 200 other seats around her.

This we do not advocate. Go a bit early, by all means, but suss out the situation first with an experienced mum. It's often the case that those who turn up last and have to stand at the back get the best view.

As for what to take with you, well, your old instamatic is going to look a trifle dated. In schools that allow filming, brace yourself for parents producing enough flashy cameras to satisfy the entire Christmas wish list of Japan.

And the final shock? Just how much your stomach will flip when your child gets up to say those lines you've rehearsed a thousand times at home. Will he remember them? Will he be sick? Will you?

At last the big moment comes. He says all ten words in the clearest, loudest, proudest voice and then gives you a virtually indiscernible thumbs up from under the baggy striped costume reserved every year for the essential role of the second shepherd. And you fill up and clap fit to burst.

For you, of course, this is a scene you've seen played out so many times. You've watched your nephews and nieces in their blurry school videos, you've seen it in church, you've even had the odd starring role in your own school days. But to him this is all new.

'I can't tell you what my Christmas play is about,' said one excited five-year-old, chosen to be narrator. 'If I tell you, you'll know how it ends and it'll spoil the surprise.' It was, of course, a traditional nativity, the greatest story ever told, told by that one little boy for the very first time and locked away in his memory forever.

TOP TIP: Should you buy your child's teacher a Christmas present? If you want to go with the crowd, then almost certainly, yes. Present-buying at Christmas and the end of the school year is common practice in most schools. It does not, however, have to be a lavish and expensive affair. Most teachers would rather have a home-made card than a pricey 'For My Teacher at Christmas' extravaganza. And a personal present, something with a link to the child, will mean more than a gift you bought and wrapped on the child's behalf. Could your child grow something, bake something, make something? Could they at least help to choose whatever you buy? Try, if you can, to steer them away from chocolates and toiletries. Most teachers get enough to set up their own tombola.

PARTY TIME

No primary school would be complete without the social whirl of the party scene.

Birthday celebrations are a big part of the social life of primary school children and, for the infants in particular, this means a plethora of party invitations. Your child will come home clutching invitations from children you've never met, inviting her to join them for the obligatory cheese sandwich, sausage on a stick and Barbie birthday cake.

It's all very flattering. In fact, if most of her class weren't at every party you go to, you could almost convince yourself of your child's immense popularity. There is, however, a downside to all this free entertainment. Unfortunately, it's going to be your child's turn to play host one day.

So terrifying a prospect is this to many parents that they lavish enormous sums on getting someone else to do it for them. They either book a meal (chicken nuggets, fish fingers, you get the picture) at one of those pubs where a pneumatic drill would struggle to be heard in the seething ball pool. Or they pay a children's entertainer a hefty fee to do that hilarious trick with the bendy magic wand, make swords from balloons and send everyone home with 'The Birdie Song' ringing in their ears.

There are other options, of course. Emigration is one, but if that sounds a little drastic you might want to take your courage in your hands and organise a do-it-yourself party – much cheaper and arguably more of a treat for children who see the bendy-wand trick at parties every other weekend.

The golden rules are:

- Don't even think about doing it at home. The money you pay to hire a hall will seem as nothing compared with the damage twenty hyped-up six-year-olds and a family-sized bag of cheesy Wotsits can do to an Axminster.
- Don't invite too many. Mothers will not snub you in the street if you omit their child's name from your list of invitees. Actually, that's not strictly true, some of them will, but it's still a risk worth taking.

Inviting the whole class, sundry relatives and the odd neighbour is too many. Unless you've had training in crowd control, your chances of keeping order are as great as the likelihood of the children favouring your home-made buns over Cadbury's Mini Rolls.

- Recruit some helpers. Most parents are more than happy to leave their children with you for a couple of hours and enjoy the peace. If you want anyone to stay and help – and we strongly recommend it – ask them in advance.

- If you're going for the standard two-hour party, go prepared for enough activities to easily fill four. Children can whip through games almost as fast as they can devour a plate of chocolate fingers. Nothing sounds more desperate than a mother looking anxiously at her watch and pleading: 'Who wants to play musical bumps again?'

- Take your lead from the children and go for a frantic pace. Pass the parcel can be one of the most dire games ever invented if you've got twenty children all waiting for the chance to win a packet of crayons. And musical statues can be a nightmare if your pedantic judge is sticking meticulously to the rules while fifteen boys who lost ten minutes ago are either play-fighting or raiding the party food.

- Think up a theme. Hide 200 tiny dinosaurs and send the children on a dinosaur hunt. Or invite the girls to dress as fairies and leave secret messages for them to find.

- Avoid the horror of the party bag. How many of us have got cupboards stuffed with whistles, spinning tops, bangles, rings, fried-egg sweets and other assorted tat which came home in party bags and was never looked at again? Invest the same money in one half-decent toy and give them a wrapped present to go home with. Children who arrived with a gift like the idea of taking one home. And, if you've got the patience, they'll like it even more if you set up a lucky dip for them to choose a present on their way out.

- Don't be too despondent if, after all those weeks of planning, your own child dissolves into tears in the second game. For most children of this age, hosting a party is often all just too much. It will, however, secure their place on the party circuit and boost their popularity among their peers. Be realistic. That may be the best you can hope for.

And, finally, if you go home traumatised, take heart. By the time your daughter is eight, she may well not want a party any more. In an era when children grow up far too soon, big parties tend to fizzle out with the move into the juniors. It'll be take-away pizzas in front of a *Friends* video before you know it. And just how depressing is that?

21 HEAD LICE, VOMITING, CHICKENPOX AND OTHER CHARMING HEALTH MATTERS

Once children are at school, a whole host of unpleasant illnesses come home with them.

They get endless colds, tummy bugs, lingering coughs, and skin rashes, which they are all too often happy to share with the rest of the family. They also develop a number of mysterious complaints that come on suddenly around 7.45 a.m. on a school morning and are miraculously cured by around 9.15.

Deciding when your child is ill enough to warrant a day off school and when they are simply fancying a day at home instead is far from easy. Only you know your child well enough to make that call.

Rest assured that whatever you decide, you'll almost certainly get it wrong sometimes. Many is the parent who, having whisked their child off to school with a chirpy: 'Come on, you'll be fine!' has felt like the worst mother in the world when the school rings an hour later to say their child has just been sick on his teacher.

By the same token, we've all been there at 10 a.m., having just begged another day off work, nursing a child who half an hour ago was shivering under the duvet and is now fancying two slices of jammy toast and a rollerblading expedition.

There are really only three golden rules.

1. Never take your supposedly sickly child to school and say to the teacher within the child's earshot: 'I've brought Joe in, but he says he's feeling unwell. *I've told him that you'll call me if he feels worse.*' As sure as eggs are eggs, the moment the maths hour starts, your child will suffer a monumental relapse and you'll be called out of work to pick him up before you can say Calpol.
2. Remember that even the most maternal teacher is still a human being. The last thing she wants to hear on the Friday before the Easter holidays is: 'Johnny's got a sickness bug. He's been sick four

times in the night. But you know Johnny; he loves school. He absolutely insisted on coming today even though we know it's very contagious. Hope you're not poorly for your skiing holiday or you'll be cursing us!'

3. Never admit to your mistakes. If the child you thought was malingering goes on to do something deeply unsavoury in assembly, feign ignorance when you go to collect him. Better to pretend you knew nothing than confess all with an: 'Actually, he did say he wasn't feeling too good, but I thought he was faking.' Not what the classroom assistant who's just spent half an hour cleaning him up really wants to hear.

INFECTIOUS DISEASES IN SCHOOLS

Children who are ill with an infectious disease should not be in school. But how long should you keep them away?

Clearly, no child should be in school until they are better, and until the risk of passing on the infection has gone. The following is a guide to help you make your decision. It is not intended to act as an aid to diagnosis – you should consult a health professional if you are in any doubt about what is making your child ill and how you should manage it.

The recommended period of time away from school is only a guide and no child should return to school until they are feeling better.

DIARRHOEA AND VOMITING ILLNESSES

Diarrhoea and/or vomiting: Recommended time off – until diarrhoea and vomiting has settled. Some schools ask that, after sickness, children do not attend school until they have had 24 vomit-free hours and are eating normally again.

RASHES AND SKIN PROBLEMS

Chickenpox: Recommended time off – five days from the onset of the rash. It is not necessary to wait until the spots have healed or crusted.

German measles: Recommended time off – five days from the onset of the rash. The child is most infectious before the diagnosis is made.

Impetigo: Recommended time off – until lesions are crusted or healed. It may be possible to shorten the time if the lesions can be kept covered.

Measles: Recommended time off – five days from the onset of the rash. Thankfully, now a rare disease, although the recent controversy over the MMR vaccine may lead to its re-emergence.

Warts and verrucas: Recommended time off – none. Affected children can go swimming, but verrucas should be covered.

OTHER ILLNESSES

Flu: Recommended time off – until the child is well. Flu is at its most infectious just before and at the onset of symptoms.

Glandular fever: Recommended time off – until the child is well.

Mumps: Recommended time off – five days from the onset of swollen glands.

Tonsillitis: Recommended time off – until the child is well.

Threadworms: Recommended time off – until the child is well. Transmission is uncommon in schools.

IMPORTANT: When deciding whether your child is well enough to return to school, it is important to bear in mind the additional risk to pregnant staff and vulnerable children. Some infections caught by a pregnant woman, such as chickenpox and German measles, can pose a danger to her baby if she is not immune. Some children also have medical conditions, such as cancer, which make them particularly vulnerable to diseases like chickenpox and measles. Do seek advice and be extra cautious if you know someone at your child's school is at an increased risk.

HEAD LICE

Head lice deserve a section all to themselves because they are, without doubt, a curse to families with young children.

Parents who are horrified when their child first gets head lice may well find that to be the first infestation of many. And, while everybody blames the problem on schools, they are in fact a problem for the whole community. Infection is common during school holidays as well as during term time. Often it stems from contact with close family and friends in the home and community, not from the school.

Head lice are small insects with six legs. They are often not much bigger than a pinhead and rarely bigger than a sesame seed. They live on or close to the scalp and have a mouth like a very small needle, which they stick into the scalp so that they can drink the host's blood.

They only live on human beings and can't be caught from animals. And it's not just children who get them – adults get them too. Itching yet? Thought so. Keep reading. There's a prevention section coming up.

HOW YOU GET THEM

The good news is that you're very unlikely to get them from brief contact with other people. Infections tend to spread from head-to-head contact with someone who has lice. They can't hop, swim, fly or jump, and it's unlikely you'd catch them from objects like a chair back.

If you catch one or two lice, they may breed and slowly increase. For the first two or three *months* you probably won't even know they're there, but then you may develop a severe itch due to an allergy rather than the bites. You may never get the itch at all and have them for *years* without even knowing it.

Nits are not the same as lice. Live lice lay eggs and stick them to the base of the hair, close to the scalp. They hatch about a week later. Nits are simply the empty egg cases. You only have head lice if you find a living, moving louse, not a nit.

PREVENTION

The best way to stop infection is for families to check their own heads. That means 'detection combing' once or twice a week so that lice are removed before they have a chance to breed. You'll need a detection comb, available from chemists.

First, wash the hair well and use a conditioner. Towel-dry it and comb it with an ordinary comb. Then switch to the detection comb and start with its teeth touching the skin of the scalp at the top of the head. Comb down to the bottom of the hair, then check the comb.

Do the same thing over and over again in all directions until the whole head is covered. It takes about ten to fifteen minutes to do it properly.

One of the best solutions is the family Bug Buster kit available from chemists. The reusable kits contain special combs designed to detect head lice. Combing wet, conditioned hair with a Bug Buster comb is considered so reliable a detection method that kits are now available on prescription for live cases.

The other option is conventional pesticides like lotions, but many parents have concerns about putting a pesticide on a child's head.

If your child does have head lice, ask about the school's policy. It may be that they will not have to be excluded from school. They've probably had them for weeks already.

And, finally, don't let head lice cause you too much anxiety. Unpleasant as they are, they rarely do any harm. An itchy scalp is usually as bad as it gets.

Still itching? So are we!

22 THE GREAT SCHOOL MEALS DEBATE

So, where do you stand on the great school meals debate?

Time was parents packed their children off to school on a Monday morning with their dinner money and never gave a second thought to what they ate during the day. If school meals were a subject for conversation at all, the traditional dialogue on the trudge home from school followed the same inevitable pattern.

'What did you do at school today?'

'Can't remember.'

'Who did you play with?'

'Don't know.'

'What did you have for lunch?'

'Forgotten.'

And forgotten it then was. Parents harking back to their own school meals of meat and two veg with the occasional dumpling thrown in either didn't think about what their children ate at lunchtime – or tried not to. When the alternative is the tedious job of making lunchboxes, it can sometimes seem best not to ask.

And then what happened? Jamie Oliver.

From the day the celebrity chef's programme about the often lamentable state of school meals was first broadcast, it became a subject impossible to ignore. Parents watched Jamie Oliver turn some poor chicken's innards into processed meat goo and recoiled in horror. Suddenly, parents didn't just *want* to know what their children had had for lunch, they were *demanding* to know. What started as a niggling worry in the back of parents' minds rose to a crescendo of concern.

Just what were their children being fed? And exactly what was inside those breadcrumb-coated children's foods that were slapped on a plate alongside a few chips and considered an acceptable meal?

What had started as a food programme rapidly became front page news. Jamie Oliver was joining the ranks of the few – the exclusive Bob Geldof club for mouthy young men who dared to confront the country's leaders and, with a bit of slang and a few expletives, force change.

And change is indeed now happening. School meals are undergoing a radical transformation. And while lots of people will tell you that it would all have happened anyway, with or without Jamie Oliver, it's an undeniable truth that he focused the nation's attention on a scandal.

Whether the changes are down to the government, school meals providers, parent pressure, inspirational school cooks or, indeed, Jamie himself hardly matters. Who takes the credit is immaterial. What really matters is what's on our children's plates.

THE CHANGES

The school meals revolution began in earnest at the beginning of 2005 when the government announced that parents would be in the front line of a new drive to improve the quality of school dinners throughout schools in England. An independent school food trust was set up and tougher standards were announced for processed foods.

By October the School Meals Review Panel had published its report. And if anyone had any doubt that school meals needed a major shake up, the title of the report – 'Turning the Tables: Transforming School Food' – pretty much acknowledged just how bad things had got. The report recommended redesigning the nation's school menus to set new minimum standards for food in schools and ensuring pupils get essential nutrients, vitamins and minerals.

The aim, according to the Government's own statement, was to reverse two decades of neglect. It threw its weight behind recommendations on setting tough minimum food-based standards as mandatory for school lunches by September 2006. The new standards will effectively ban poor quality foods, high in fat, salt and sugar, and reformed or reconstituted foods made from that most unappetizing of all ingredients, meat slurry.

The Government is also backing recommendations to introduce even more stringent standards, stipulating the essential nutrients, vitamins and minerals needed for school meals in primary schools by no later than 2008, and secondary schools no later than the following year.

And it hopes to improve the next generation's diets by aiming to put a greater emphasis on teaching 11 to 14-year-old pupils practical cooking skills in secondary schools.

The government claims to be investing £220m over three years to help schools and local education authorities transform school meals through training and increased hours for cooks, equipment and a minimum spend on ingredients – 50p at primary schools, 60p at secondary schools.

So has parent power played its part in the promised improvements?

When the 'Turning the Tables' report was launched, Suzi Leather, chair of the School Meals Review Panel, said this: 'Not since the creation of the welfare state has there been such a groundswell of public support for improvement of school meals.'

I'd take that for a yes.

THE BAD OLD DAYS (I.E. A COUPLE OF YEARS AGO)

Were things really ever as bad as we were led to believe or was it all media hype? Well, generally speaking, things had got pretty dire.

No doubt, there were saintly schools managing nutritious home-cooked foods for a song, and there were certainly many already on the path to changing for the better, but there were still others serving children a diet of, well, frankly who knows? One of life's great mysteries is exactly what does go into a dish with a zingy title and minimal clues as to what might be inside.

It wasn't all bad, far from it. In fact, some of your old favourites from school dinners of the past were still there. Irish stew and dumplings, home-made chicken pie, toad in the hole – bet you can smell it now.

The trouble was that often children were given a choice and young children with choices can be a very bad combination indeed. Chicken nuggets or fresh spring salad; roast bacon and pineapple or processed turkey shape; shepherd's pie or sausage roll. All too often, children opted for the convenience food while the stew and dumplings were left congealing in the pan.

So why did children make such bad choices? Well, doubtless there were plenty of the kind of children Jamie encountered on his programme to whom 'Broccoli Floret' sounded like a new cookery teacher for Horrid Henry.

Then there were the fussy eaters whose parents were demented daily by the trial of getting their offspring to eat so much as a spoonful of peas. Would these children willingly opt for egg salad when the alternative was chips, sausage roll and gravy? Er, no.

And there's that other big influence – the archetypal 'children's meal' served all too often in pubs, cafes and restaurants the length and breadth of the land. While, when parents are dining out, they get to choose nutritious, adventurous, freshly cooked food from an extensive menu, what are children offered? Chicken nuggets, fish fingers, sausages or a burger with, if you're lucky, a few exciting freebies – some cheap crayons to keep the kids 'entertained' between courses and a free ice-cream of such dubious quality that it's all ice and no cream.

Ask if they can have a small portion of an adult's dish and the waiter will look at you as if you've just shown the first signs of madness. 'But, surely, madam, this is a *child*. You wouldn't want our chef to waste his talents and good nutrients on a *child*.'

So children come to equate dining out with eating rubbish. Small wonder that when they're offered rubbish when mum isn't around to supervise, it's the tasty, familiar, fun-shaped food they go for.

By advocating that children should be given a choice of healthy options, and nothing but healthy options, Jamie Oliver effectively forced their hand. He also, very cleverly, forced the hand of parents, too.

Mums who railed against the changes, who insisted they wouldn't be dictated to, were often won over not so much by the healthy eating arguments as by a simple fact – in my experience, no parent has yet been born who loved making pack-ups.

SCHOOL MEALS v PACKED LUNCHES

So, school meals or packed lunches? It's a tricky one.

If school meals are going to become as good as they claim, surely everyone will opt for a good old school dinner. And maybe not.

Bad publicity about the state of school dinners has actually driven many parents away. The debate led lots of parents to dust off the lunchboxes, ironically at a time when standards were finally rising. There was also the fact that children brought up on convenience foods weren't always rampant with enthusiasm when the likes of chicken fricassee and lamb hotpot started appearing on their plates.

They went home and moaned to mum. Mum said something along the lines of: 'I'm not paying for you to have food you don't like.' Or took the sympathetic line: 'He hasn't had a thing to eat. He's been hungry all day. I don't know why they don't go back to what they used to give them. He used to love his school dinners.'

But while some quit school dinners altogether, many a parent put the flags out at the prospect of better food on their children's plates. It might not be perfect, but it's certainly better than it was.

The hope is that by driving up standards, in the long term more parents will be tempted to give school meals a try and that children, particularly the disadvantaged, will get what school dinners were always supposed to be – at least one good meal a day.

In the meantime, large numbers of children are relying on their parents to make sensible decisions about what goes into their lunchboxes. And if you saw what went into some of them, you'd start to wonder whether chicken goo was such a bad idea after all.

The switch to packed lunches has been a mixed blessing. Just as a cooked school dinner can be good or bad, so a pack-up can be either packed with goodness – or a nutritionist's worst nightmare. It is, after all, quite possible to make an entire lunchbox consisting basically of salt, fat and sugar. Jam sandwiches, sausage rolls, cheese straws, chocolate biscuits, crisps, sweets, fizzy drinks. A healthier alternative to school dinners? Hardly.

The trouble is that, for busy parents, packing the school lunch box is an end-of-the-day (or, worst still, 8 a.m.) horror. It is just so tempting to fill up a hungry child with all those bits of rubbish straight off the supermarket shelf that make lunch boxes a relative doddle.

Who hasn't sometimes resorted to processed cheese that looks like a distant relative of Bostik, or slapped uniform squares of ham that wouldn't look out of place at the Early Learning Centre between rubbery slices of white bread? And just how easy is it to persuade your child that his raw carrot and raisins are a good idea when he has to eat his lunch surrounded by the unmistakable waft of his neighbours' cheesy puffs?

The bottom line is that if, for whatever reason, we opt out of school meals, the onus for giving our children a nutritious midday meal falls on us. It's no good complaining about what schools provide if what we provide ourselves is considerably worse.

And, if you are sticking with DIY lunches, two things should console you as you stuff your child's lunchbox with fruit, tuna, wholemeal bread and raw veg. The first is that he'll be getting a healthier lunch than his crisp-munching, pop-slurping, sweet-chewing neighbours. And the second is that when he lifts the lunchbox lid in the school dining hall tomorrow lunchtime, you won't be there to take the flak.

TIPS FOR TEMPTING LUNCHBOXES

- Sandwiches don't have to be boring. Just varying the kind of bread you choose might make a healthy filling look more tempting. Try pitta bread, bagels, tortillas and mini bread buns to make a dull lunchbox look more enticing.
- Try mixing some of the fillings. Tuna, sweetcorn and cucumber make a good granary bread filling, and chicken salad is great in a tortilla wrap.
- Fed up of sandwiches? Try cooked pasta or rice with vegetables, fish or beans.
- Let your child choose their own fruit – and don't be limited to apples and bananas. Lunchboxes are also perfect for cherry tomatoes, peaches, plums, melon slices, kiwi, cherries, satsumas, pears, grapes and strawberries. A fruit salad, made with chunks of fruit and apple juice, makes a scrumptious addition to a lunchbox.
- And what about raisins, dried apricots, cheese chunks, yogurt, bread sticks and a healthy dip, fruit cake or carrot cake?
- Drink, anyone? Avoid fizzy and sugary drinks which can damage children's teeth. Pure fruit juice contains vitamins but also has acid that can cause tooth decay – best limited to meal times. Other options are fruit smoothies, made by blending fruit, milk and yogurt together. And, of course, don't forget milk. Arguably the best option is also the cheapest – water!

> 'Two years ago, I wouldn't have entertained the idea of giving my children school dinners. I like to know what they're eating and feeding them convenience foods at the cheapest possible price isn't my idea of a healthy lunch. Now, I look at the school menus and look at what goes into their lunchboxes and I seriously wonder whether I'm still doing the right thing.'
>
> *A mum*

23 REGIONAL DIFFERENCES

Regional variations mean that there are some differences in what is provided by education authorities all over England. No two schools are alike, let alone two education authorities.

But by far the biggest differences are in Scotland, Wales and Ireland. Some of the variations are subtle, others more radical. Here, we outline some of the more obvious differences. For full details, contact your local education provider.

SCOTLAND

In the state system, young children in Scotland follow a flexible curriculum for three- to five-year-olds. A free, part-time, pre-school place is available for every three- and four-year-old.

Children can start later than their counterparts in England, depending on which month they were born. They normally enter school in the August when they are aged between four and a half and five and a half and go into Primary One, which equates to a reception year.

Children must start no later than the August after their fifth birthday. But children born between September and February can start school in the August preceding their fifth birthday, or can choose to defer to the following August.

They then usually follow a seven-year programme of education and move on to secondary school in the August when they are between eleven and a half and twelve and a half.

All schools produce an annual handbook giving full details about themselves, including details of attainment at the school. Information on all schools, including links to inspection reports and school websites, is also available at www.parentzonescotland.gov.uk. There are no published league tables.

Schools are also subject to a system of inspection, and reports on recently inspected schools are available from HM Inspectorate of Education.

Education authorities normally offer school places to children on the basis of catchment areas. But parents can request a place at a school outside their catchment area by submitting a 'placing request' to their education authority. If there are more requests than places available, the authority will allocate places according to laid-down criteria. Parents have a right of appeal.

There are state denominational schools in some parts of Scotland, mostly Roman Catholic.

Following extensive consultation in 2002 with the people of Scotland on the state of school education, there was a commitment to reviewing the curriculum from age 3 to 18.

A review group was set up and produced a report which recommended what parents had asked for - a less cluttered curriculum offering more choice and enjoyment. The new curriculum is now on its way.

Changes are also taking place for children with special needs. A new bill from the Scottish Executive has replaced the Record of Needs system. The new parent-friendly support plan helps children with 'additional support needs'.

WALES

Three- and four-year-olds are entitled to a free early education place.

Wales has adopted a different curriculum. The National Curriculum for Wales was introduced in all schools in 2000 and offers greater flexibility to teachers.

New proposals are also being examined for children in the foundation stage of education – ultimately from three to seven years. The emphasis will be on learning through well-structured play, practical activity and investigation. The aim is for full implementation by 2008.

National testing for Key Stage 1 was scrapped in Welsh schools from spring 2002. And tests for eleven- and fourteen-year-olds will be phased out by 2007/8. All testing will be replaced by teacher assessments and a new skills test for ten-year-olds focusing on numeracy, literacy and problem solving.

Nearly all infant classes have thirty or fewer pupils and the aim is to reduce that further. Classes for juniors are also being reduced to thirty or under. The average primary class size is now less than 25. Policies for admissions to school are determined annually.

The National Assembly for Wales has stopped publishing schools' results, though they are still published in individual school prospectuses.

The Assembly also now has powers to secure regional provision for children with special educational needs.

NORTHERN IRELAND

In Northern Ireland many three- and four-year-olds are entitled to a pre-school education place. This may be in voluntary playgroups (part-time places only) or in nursery schools or classes (some of which offer full-time places only, some part-time only and some both full- and part-time).

The cut-off point for school admissions is the end of June. That means that children who turn four before the end of June will start school two months later in September. Children born in July and August will be five when they start – so they will be the oldest in the class, not the youngest.

Each school has its own admissions criteria, set down by its board of governors.

Primary education is dominated by two categories of school: controlled schools and Catholic maintained schools. Together they account for approximately 95% of all primary school enrolments. The remainder is accounted for by integrated primary schools. The Department of Education is committed to encouraging more integrated education so that children of different faiths can study together.

Schools follow the Northern Ireland Curriculum, which sets down a number of areas of study, and children study in two key stages – Key Stage 1 covers school years One to Four for pupils aged four to eight, Key Stage 2 covers school years Five to Seven for pupils aged eight to eleven. The compulsory subjects studied in primary schools are English, maths, science and technology, history, geography, physical education, art and design, music, religious education and Irish in Irish-speaking schools.

In addition, at primary level there are four compulsory cross-curricular themes: information technology, education for mutual understanding

(EMU), cultural heritage and health education. These themes are not subjects in their own right but are taught through the compulsory subjects of the curriculum. Following a review, the Northern Ireland Council for the Curriculum, Examinations and Assessment has forwarded proposals for a revised curriculum.

Performance tables have been abolished, but schools are subject to a system of inspection by the Education and Training Inspectorate and their reports are available to parents.

By far the biggest difference in Northern Ireland's education system is that children still sit an eleven-plus test before moving on to a grammar school or secondary school.

That system is to be scrapped in 2008 and replaced with new arrangements. The key concept of the new arrangements is an Entitlement Framework which will give pupils access to a minimum number and range of courses – including, for the first time, a choice of vocational courses – regardless of what school they attend, or where they live.

Transfer from primary to post-primary school will be based on parental choice, informed by a pupil profile and better information about the options available to best meet the individual pupil's needs, aspirations, abilities and interests.

24 CHOOSING A SECONDARY SCHOOL

The big difference between choosing a school the first time around and the second is that there's an extra opinion to take into account.

You can pore all you like over the Ofsted reports and performance tables, but be braced for all your research and logic to be knocked off course by one strong voice in the background – that of your child.

And will he be worrying about the school's GCSE results? Oh, no. He'll want to go to Kingston High because '*all* of my friends are going there and anyway they all say that Trinity is rubbish'. Get out of that one, mum.

The fact is that choosing a secondary school is a complicated business and it's getting more complicated by the day. The only sensible way forward is to shop around, just as you did for your child's first school, and see if you can't cajole your child into a compromise decision that puts more emphasis on his strengths and requirements than his friendships.

And do bear in mind that, if you have more than one child, you may well want to send them all to the same school. Some parents do choose whichever schools suit their individual children best, but most want all their children to attend the same school. In that case, you may be looking for the best school for all your children, not the one that suits the eldest best.

Secondary education in England is currently undergoing big changes. What it should mean for your child is that by the time they start making the kind of choices that could affect their future careers, they should – theoretically – be able to embark on a school timetable tailor-made to suit them and their vision for the future.

Gone are some of the old rules that tied up a big chunk of their learning with subjects they had to study. The changes mean that the only main compulsory subjects will be maths, English, science, PE, religious education, and information and communication technology. After that, they get largely a free choice, which opens up far more of their school day for them to study subjects they enjoy. They have the opportunity to specialise much earlier in areas where they have particular skills and where their future studies and careers might lie.

To add to the complications, schools are also specialising more. By taking on special status, they get a big injection of cash to invest in a particular area of learning. You might well find that the schools in your area have got fancy new titles and are now calling themselves colleges specialising in subjects including technology, performing arts and sport.

In theory, at least, it sounds a perfectly sensible idea. Your child, the budding Nicole Kidman, signs up for the school with special status in performing arts and gets the benefit of their added facilities and expertise.

In practice, of course, nothing in education is ever quite so simple. Some of the schools that specialise (and most soon will) are generally allowed to select up to 10% of their pupils based on aptitude. So, for instance, a child with a real flare for drama could secure a place in a school specialising in drama no matter where he lived. That's the theory. In reality, many schools still choose their pupils the way they always did. If the school is particularly popular, it's still more likely to be where the child lives than what he's good at which secures him a place.

In some rural areas, of course, there may well be only one school your child could realistically attend anyway.

So don't be too blinded by a school's special status. Even schools that specialise in a subject your child isn't interested in should still offer a good education and a wide curriculum covering all the usual subjects.

The best way to choose a secondary school is the same way you chose your child's primary school – going round and seeing for yourself.

HOW TO CHOOSE A SECONDARY SCHOOL

The first rule is to be open-minded. Many good schools cannot get parents even to walk through the door because of an often-unjustified reputation.

Don't just go to the open day of the school you like the sound of. Go to all the open days of all the schools that you could reasonably put on your shortlist. It might not be the one at the top of your list that impresses you most.

And what should you be looking for above all else? Enthusiasm. Talk to the teachers. Talk particularly to the teachers of the subjects your child likes best. Do they seem genuinely fired up? Do you get the feeling that they have a real love for their subject? The teachers who come over as bubbling with enthusiasm are the teachers you want teaching your child. Enthusiasm is infectious – and it's worth a dozen new computers.

So, what then? You've done your tour of the open days and you make your decision? Wrong.

After the open days, pick your favourite – maybe more than one – and ask for a tour of the school on a normal school day. Get permission to take your child with you.

Ask to go around the classrooms and see what the school is like day to day. Get a feel for the place, for what it's like to be a pupil there. Do the pupils look interested, keen, involved in the lessons? What's the behaviour like? Could you see your child fitting in?

Meet the head. Talk to him or her about the ethos of the school. Ask what their school could do for your child. Ask particularly about what the school is able to offer around the age of fourteen when your child will be making those crucial timetable choices. How flexible will his options be?

Then come away and talk it through with your child. See if you can come to a decision based on what's best for him, not what most suits his best friend. At the end of the day, it could all come down to your powers of persuasion and your child's personality. Yes, you're probably right in saying that he'll soon make new friends at a new school. But be warned. If your child really digs his heels in, he wouldn't be the first to go to a new school determined to be miserable just to prove a point.

> If I was looking for a school for my child, I'd be going along to the open evenings and having conversations with the teachers. If what you pick up is a sense of enthusiasm, that feeling of passion for their subject, then that's what they'll put over to the children in their lessons, and that's what good teaching is all about.
>
> *A secondary school head*

Once they're happily settled in their secondary school, you can breathe a sigh of relief at the end of a job well done. Except that then, of course, there are more SATs coming along, GCSEs, A levels, universities to choose, and so it goes relentlessly on.

Yes, education is hugely important, but never lose sight of the fact that the most important thing of all is *your* child. In the push and rush of tests and targets, of reports and results, always remember that these years with a young child are precious indeed. Make time to enjoy them, every precious one.

INDEX